The Periodical Context
of English Literature
1708-1907

By
Daniel Fader

Department of English

University of Michigan

University Microfilms

A Xerox Company

Ann Arbor, Michigan 48106

1971

Contents

Preface

All of us who teach English literature to students at any level from high school freshmen through college seniors have occasionally felt that we build monuments on friable land. My own most recent experience of this came while teaching Shakespeare to college sophomores and juniors. We were reading *Julius Caesar* and I was speaking of modern man's well developed sense of time, his awareness of chronology, and his high consciousness of anachronism. To illustrate my point, I invited the class to turn to Act II, scene one, page 28 in the Washington Square Press edition, and to identify the famous anachronism on that page. One hundred and six students read the thirty lines on the page; one hundred and six pairs of empty eyes returned my enquiring gaze.

The passage I sent them to is Brutus's first meeting with Cassius' band of conspirators. Trebonius adds his voice to Brutus's in denying that Mark Antony must also be assassinated. The clock strikes. Brutus says, "Peace! Count the clock;" Cassius responds, "The clock has stricken three;" and not one of my students questioned the presence of a striking clock in first century Rome.

A similar experience came to me as guest lecturer in a Michigan high school. My subject was *The Merchant of Venice,* my audience a group of juniors and seniors from three English classes. We were talking about Shylock when I had a sudden sense of dislocation. Had we read the same play? I asked the question I should have asked earlier: "Does Shakespeare want his audience to *dislike* Shylock?" I shall never forget the answering analogy made by one hip and articulate young lady:

"Shylock is like black people in America. Shakespeare knew the Jew wasn't getting fair treatment in the Renaissance just the way anybody writing now knows that black people are persecuted. Shakespeare wants us to sympathize with Shylock. And we do. [pause, then emphatically] Anyway, *I* do."

For the rest of that hour and for part of the next I tried to reconstruct some of the attitudes and assumptions of the Renaissance man. As I spoke about Renaissance medicine and psychology, I watched their faces; their expressions and questions made me realize how wrong I had been. The ground was strong enough, but the base of the monument was disastrously weak. And that was attributable entirely to the builder, not to the materials.

As builder, I had spoken and believed customary words about architectural relationships between literature and contemporary context. But the words were merely duty; I had lost—perhaps I had never known—the impact of their meaning. This project is one result of directly experiencing that impact.

The heart of the project is thirty-nine English periodicals whose every page has been put upon microfilm. Thirty-nine periodicals published in England between 1708 and 1907 is a very small number when compared with the thousands that were created and expired during those two hundred years. The three hundred and fifty thousand pages which compose these chosen periodicals are hardly more than a tittle when compared with tens of millions written and published in the eighteenth and nineteenth centuries. But if they bulk small, they loom extraordinarily large in the long history of English periodical publication.

The relative importance of these journals and magazines (none are newspapers in the modern sense of that word) lies both in their contents and their contributors. Twenty-three of the thirty-nine are edited by men famous in English letters. The twenty-three represent fifteen different individuals who use the pages of periodical literature for everything from a practice ground to a repository for their works. Their names form a galaxy of stars with attendant satellites: Joseph Addison, Richard Steele, Daniel Defoe, Jonathan Swift, Henry Fielding, Tobias Smollett, Oliver Goldsmith, Samuel Johnson, Lord Byron, Leigh Hunt, Charles Dickens, Anthony Trollope, W. M. Rossetti, Arthur Symons, and Aubrey Beardsley.

Bear in mind that this is a list of editors. Though all fifteen are contributors as well, all famous contributors are not editors. During the course of this essay, whose aim is to enrich the teaching of English literature by providing a vital context for its monuments, I will identify some of those contributors. But my main purpose will be to weave the important work of eighteenth and nineteenth century literary figures into the fabric of periodical literature which is the adornment of the times.

I

Just as no one can read widely in eighteenth century English literature without including the periodical writings of Addison and Steele, no one can hope to understand the era without reading the *Tatler, Spectator,* and *Guardian.* Walter Graham, in his good book *English Literary Periodicals,* writes of Addison's and Steele's unique place in English literature: "Unlike all their predecessors and most of their followers, Steele and Addison earned their niche in the halls of literary fame solely by their periodical writing. In the *Tatler, Spectator,* and *Guardian,* journalism and literature were first brought into happy union."

Graham may not be doing entire justice to either man's importance in the theatre—Addison's *Cato,* a tragedy played in 1713, was a great success and is still readable; Steele's comedies such as *The Funeral* (1701) and *The Conscious Lovers* (1722) helped make and confirm contemporary theatrical taste—but he is right about the new relationship between journalism and literature which has its English roots in the *Tatler* and *Spectator.* Graham is also right when he goes against modern habit by speaking of "Steele and Addison," in contrast to customary twentieth century usage which gives precedence to Joseph Addison.

Addison gives place to Steele in Graham's phrase because it is Steele who is founder and guiding force behind *The Tatler* (1709-11), earliest of the great English periodicals. Richard Steele was born in 1672, as was his good friend Addison; both are at Charterhouse together, and both go up to Oxford where they matriculate at separate colleges. Steele, the lesser talent, is first known by his treatise of 1701 called "The

Christian Hero." Of small literary value, the work is important because of what it signals rather than what it is. As "An Argument proving that no Principles but those of Religion are Sufficient to make a great Man," Steele's essay points away from the easy morality of the Restoration and toward the reformed manners and morals of the eighteenth century. It is especially significant for its advocacy of chivalry toward women, an attitude which pervades Steele's periodical writing as well as most of the literature of the next half-century and beyond.

Steele does not set a variable course. Having once found congenial direction, he holds to it for the first three decades of the eighteenth century. By the time of his death in 1729, he has contributed greatly to replacing the Restoration drama of elastic morality with the eighteenth century theatre of decorum. *The Funeral,* which develops the pattern of two rational couples politely adventuring toward a happy and respectable conclusion, embodies in more-or-less dramatic form the critical dictum of *Tatler* No. 182: the only acceptable sort of play demonstrates "all the reverend offices of life preserved with the utmost care." But it is not until *The Conscious Lovers,* in which Steele manages to support his principle with such appeal and (by this time) so much authority, that the gay couple of imperfect morality permanently becomes a relic of the Restoration stage.

In beginning *The Tatler,* Steele has help from his good friend Jonathan Swift. Something of Swift darkens the customary measured civility of Steele in his prefatory statement to the first collected volume: "The general purpose of this paper is to expose the false arts of life, to pull off the disguises of cunning, vanity, and affectation, and to recommend a general simplicity in our dress, our discourse, and our behavior." But if there are traces of Swift, there's nothing yet of Addison who is pursuing a political career in Ireland as secretary to the Lieutenant General.

Graham's ordering of Steele and Addison is further justified by the fact that Steele writes 188 of the thrice-weekly *Tatlers* (Tuesday, Thursday, and Saturday; days when the London post ventures into the countryside) and collaborates with Addison on 36, while Addison is solely responsible for 42 numbers. John Gay, famous for his *Beggar's Opera* (1728) and its sequel *Polly* (1729), and a contributor to Steele's *Guardian* (1713), regards the Steele papers as the heart of *The Tatler.* He writes in his *Present State of Wit,* published in 1711, the following praise:

> It would have been a jest some time since, for a man to have asserted that any thing witty could be said in praise of a married state; or that devotion and virtue were any way necessary to the character of a fine gentleman...[Bickerstaff's] writings have set all our wits and men of letters upon a new way of thinking, of which they had little or no notion before; and though we cannot yet say that any of them have come up to the beauties of the original, I think we may venture to affirm, that every one of them writes and thinks much more justly than they did some time since.

The "Bickerstaff" to whom Gay refers is that same Isaac Bickerstaff of whom Ricardo Quintana writes in *The Mind and Art of Jonathan Swift:* "When on 12 April 1709 Steele began to issue his *Tatler,* he could think of no better means to ensure its popularity than by assuming the character of Isaac Bickerstaff [Swift], author of the 'Predictions for the Year 1708' and their famous sequels." Swift's ironic pamphlets on the death of the astrologer Partridge were as popular as they were entertaining; even so, they are outdone by the new character of Bickerstaff.

Writing in the next century, Hippolyte Taine, the French historian, comments that "It is no small thing to make morality fashionable." It is indeed no small thing that Steele does with the *nom de plume* of Isaac Bickerstaff. Sensing and leading the change toward decorum and away from impropriety, he publishes his "lucubrations" on the fine and fitting preoccupations of the Christian gentleman. With their appearance in *The Tatler,* the modern English periodical may be said to begin.

Joseph Addison lives ten years less than Richard Steele and is, rather unjustly, ten times more famous. Before the

Spectator papers of 1711-12, his best known work is a long poem in heroic couplets which sings Marlborough's victory at Blenheim. Called "The Campaign" (1704), it is so well received by the government that Addison is appointed Under-Secretary of State from 1706 to 1708. An accomplished classical scholar, his Latin poetry is still praised and his study of classical prose seems to be one considerable factor in producing his remarkably pleasant English style.

That his study of classical prose influences his own style is only conjectural, but what is not speculative, is the influence of Addison's style upon his contemporaries and admirers for the next hundred years. An intelligent, comprehensive study of modern English prose style remains to be written. When it is written, it will pause in its slow movement from the sixteenth through the twentieth century to pay Addison his due; when it does, it can hardly do better than to quote Samuel Johnson's tribute at the end of his *Life of Addison:*

His prose is the model of the middle style; on grave subjects not formal, on light occasions not groveling; pure without scrupulosity, and exact without apparent elaboration; always equable, and always easy, without glowing words or pointed sentences. Addison never deviates from his track to snatch a grace; he seeks no ambitious ornaments, and tries no hazardous innovations. His page is always luminous, but never blazes in unexpected splendour.

It was apparently his principal endeavor to avoid all harshness and severity of diction....what he attempted, he performed; he is never feeble, and he did not wish to be energetick; he is never rapid, and he never stagnates. His sentences have neither studied amplitude, nor affected brevity; his periods, though not dilligently rounded, are voluble and easy. Whoever wishes to attain an English style, familiar but not coarse, and elegant but not ostentatious, must give his days and nights to the volumes of Addison.

The voluble, easy, familiar, and elegant Addison of whom Johnson writes is primarily the Addison of the *Spectator* papers. What Steele was to *The Tatler,* Addison is to *The Spectator.* Though in number his contributions are almost matched by those of Steele, in quality they are unequalled. Johnson's considered praise is based upon examples of Addison's prose style like that found in *Spectator* No. 10, published on Monday, March 12, 1711:

> It is with much satisfaction that I hear this great city enquiring day by day after these my papers and receiving my morning lectures with a becoming seriousness and attention. My publisher tells me that there are already three thousand of them distributed every day [circulation actually got above 20,000 a day, a remarkable figure for the time]....Since I have raised to myself so great an audience, I shall spare no pains to make their instruction agreeable and their diversion useful. For which reasons I shall endeavor to enliven morality with wit, and to temper wit with morality....I have resolved to refresh their memories from day to day, till I have recovered them out of that desperate state of vice and folly into which the age is fallen....It was said of Socrates that he brought philosophy down from Heaven, to inhabit among men; and I shall be ambitious to have it said of me, that I have brought philosophy out of closets and libraries, schools and colleges, to dwell in clubs and assemblies, at tea-tables and in coffeehouses.

> I would therefore in a very particular manner recommend these my speculations to all well-regulated families, that set apart an hour in every morning for tea and bread and butter; and would earnestly advise them for their good to order this paper to be punctually served up, and to be looked upon as part of the tea equipage.

Prose like this is still a rare thing at the beginning of the eighteenth century. Simple eloquence is rare enough in any time; but it is even more to be prized in a world only a century removed from Ciceronian and Tacitean extremes of fullness and brevity. The middle style wins out, and Addison is the direct inheritor of John Dryden (to whose translation of Virgil he is allowed to contribute while a Fellow of Magdalen College at Oxford), but the struggle is by no means concluded when Addison deeply influences its course. Not only does he temper wit and morality each with equal measure of the other, but he tempers indecorous English prose to fit an age of moderation.

Addison is so thoroughly if wittily preoccupied with morality and moderation that he deserves C. S. Lewis's apt characterization of him as the epitome of Victorian. Writing in his "Addison" essay, Lewis points out the various qualities apart from style that distinguish the *Spectator* and he identifies their essentially Victorian nature. Addison is not all Good Form, but he would not be himself without it. He is full of vague religious sensibilities, he is gently but firmly patronizing of women, he is enviable in his sense of all's right with the world, and he invariably perceives the world through its need for his lessoning.

Addison is surely the archetypal Victorian; he is also a great stylist and a memorable contributor to the theory of literary criticism. Undoubtedly his most original work in the area is included within eleven *Spectator* papers beginning with number 411 and ending with 421. In these brilliant essays Addison accomplishes the considerable feat of expanding the customary criteria for evaluating art. Before Addison, men speak of "beauty" when measuring their pleasure in the artist's work, and beauty is all. After Addison, beauty is not enough. Henceforth, men deal with notions of sublimity—by which Addison means spiritual dimension, or greatness—and novelty, both of which become essential standards of judgment for Romantic criticism.

Addison is not all sublimity and beauty. When moved by sufficient cause, he can be a formidable enemy. In the inflamed days of 1713, with the nation bitterly divided over the question of royal succession, Addison the Whig uses his pen to assassinate the character of the Tory editor whose *Mercator* or *Commerce Retriev'd* (1713-14) supports Tory ideas of trade: "[He is] a false, shuffling, prevaricating rascal...unqualified to give his testimony in a Court of Justice." The name of the rascal is Daniel Defoe.

In 1702, when Defoe is 42 years of age and already twice a bankrupt, he publishes "The Shortest Way with the Dissenters," an ironical defense of the rabid Anglicans who want to force conformation to the Church upon Dissenting Englishmen. Unfortunately, readers on both sides entirely miss the intended irony, all men become his sworn enemies, and the government orders his arrest for sedition. Defoe becomes a fugitive; the following description is included within an advertisement for his arrest published in *The London Gazette* of 7-11 January, 1703: "[Defoe is] a middle-sized spare man, about 40 years old, of a brown complexion, and dark brown coloured hair, but wears a wig; [he has] a hooked nose, a sharp chin, grey eyes, and a mould near his mouth...."

Defoe is apparently no more fortunate than handsome, for he is apprehended, convicted, pilloried, and subsequently jailed. After spending seven months of the year 1703 in jail, he is released through the intervention of Robert Harley, later Earl of Oxford and the man most responsible for the peaceful settling of the British crown upon George I and the House of Hanover. Defoe becomes Harley's man; in that capacity, though secretly, he undertakes to write the thrice-weekly *Review of the Affairs of France* (1704-13). During this decade, with England and France at war, Defoe writes a politico-economic pamphlet of four quarto pages published about one hundred and fifty times a year *entirely by himself.* His long term purpose is to further British trade. Almost by the way he effectively promotes the Union with Scotland (1707) and masters a journalistic style which will later be the making of him as novelist.

By 1719, after serving various governments in secret capacities—often posing as the enemy, he manages to edit and control opposition periodicals—Defoe has outlived his public usefulness and finds himself approaching sixty both unemployed and unemployable in his life-long profession of journalist. His bad luck is the world's good fortune for he becomes by necessity a novelist, one of the best and most prolific storytellers of his or any other time.

Some critics debate Defoe's right to the title of novelist, pointing out that it is not realism but authenticity that he strives to obtain. They refer not only to his exhaustive descriptions but also to the fact that he keeps his name from the title page of his books because he wants them to be accepted as memoirs of real people. Ian Watt, writing in *The Rise of the Novel,* identifies this very search for authenticity as a significant characteristic of the new fiction:

> Defoe would seem to be the first of our writers who visualized the whole of his narrative as though it occurred in an actual physical environment. His attention to the description of milieu is still intermittent; but occasional vivid details supplement the continual implication of his narrative and make us attach Robinson Crusoe and Moll Flanders much more completely to their environments than is the case with previous fictional characters. Characteristically, this solidity of setting is particularly noticeable in Defoe's treatment of movable objects in the physical world: in *Moll Flanders* there is much linen and gold to be counted, while Robinson Crusoe's island is full of memorable pieces of clothing and hardware.

Furthermore, says Watt, a proper and characteristic aim of the novelist is one which he shares with the philosopher— "the production of what purports to be an authentic account of the actual experiences of individuals." Had Watt wished to make wider application of this shared purpose, he might have noted that it is the chief aim of the journalist as well.

Defoe the editorializing journalist is at all times visible in the person of Defoe the preaching novelist. He uses his man Crusoe as an object lesson in disobedience to family and Maker: Crusoe departs his proper place in life and is caused thereafter often to tell his readers that he is "the most miserable wretch that ever was born." In *Moll Flanders* and *Journal of the Plague Year* (both 1722) Defoe breaks his narratives to attend respectively to the desirability of an orphan's asylum and the cruel nature of quarantine. Books like *A New Voyage Round the World* (1724) and *The Four Voyages of Captain George Roberts* (1726) editorialize on the sharp and ungentlemanly trading practices of foreigners. The geographic, historic, and human details which abound in all his works are clearly the result of omnivorous journalistic reading and observance of life.

Perhaps the most significant relationship between Defoe's twenty years of training as journalist and his subsequent decade as novelist is the essentially journalistic nature of *Robinson Crusoe* and *Moll Flanders,* the two works for which he is best remembered. Both claim to be confessional autobiography, a kind of journalism of the self. As in Dickens' novels, the modern reader notices the episodic nature of the narrative. While Dickens actually writes his novels for serial publication, Defoe is simply an incorrigible journalist, creating narratives out of fragments, molding his novels out of the bits and pieces of daily life.

As Richard Steele and Joseph Addison make a convenient pair of journalists for purposes of comparison and contrast, so do Daniel Defoe and Jonathan Swift. Though Defoe is seven years older than Swift, and precedes him in death by fourteen years, both are journalists and writers of fiction during approximately the same years of the eighteenth century. In October 1710, for example, when Defoe is in the midst of writing his famous *Review,* Swift undertakes the writing and editing of a new Tory periodical called *The Examiner.* For the few months of its existence before Swift's stewardship, it is thoroughly unremarkable. For the thirty-odd numbers he either writes or edits, *The Examiner* becomes a weapon without equal in the government's armory. *Examiner* No. 15, containing an essay entitled "The Art of Political Lying" and published during the first week of November, 1910, epitomizes Swift's savage art; here is a part of that essay:

> I am prevailed on, through the importunity of friends, to interrupt the scheme I had begun in my last paper, by an Essay upon the Art of Political Lying. We are told, "the Devil is the father of lies,

and was a liar from the beginning; so that beyond contradiction, the invention is old: And which is more, his first essay of it was purely political, employed in undermining the authority of his Prince, and seducing a third part of the subjects from their obedience. For which he was driven down from Heaven, where (as Milton expresseth it) he had been viceroy of a great western province; and forced to exercise his talent in inferior regions among other fallen spirits, or poor deluded men, whome he still daily tempts to his own sin, and will ever do so till he is chained in the bottomless pit.

But though the Devil be the father of lies, he seems, like other great inventors, to have lost much of his reputation, by the continual improvements that have been made upon him.

Who first reduced lying into an art, and adapted it to politics, is not so clear from history, though I have made some diligent enquiries; I shall therefore consider it only according to the modern system, as it has been cultivated these twenty years past in the southern part of our own island.

The poets tell us, that after the giants were overthrown by the gods, the earth in revenge produced her last offspring, which was Fame. And the fable is thus interpreted; that when tumults and seditions are quieted, rumours and false reports are plentifully spread through a nation. So that by this account, *lying* is the last relief of a routed, earth-born, rebellious party in a state. But here, the moderns have made great additions, applying this art to the gaining of power, and preserving it, as well as revenging themselves after they have lost it: as the same instruments are made use of by animals to feed themselves when they are hungry, and bite those that tread upon them.

But the same genealogy cannot always be admitted for *political lying;* I shall therefore desire to refine upon it, by adding some circumstances of its birth and parents. A political lie is sometimes born out of a discarded statesman's head, and thence delivered to be nursed and dandled by the mob. Sometimes, it is produced a monster and *licked* into shape; at other times it comes into the world completely formed, and is spoiled in the licking. It is often born an infant in the regular way, and requires time to mature it: and often it sees the light in its full growth, but dwindles away by degree. Sometimes it is of noble birth; and sometimes the spawn of a stock-jobber. *Here,* it screams aloud at the opening of the womb; and *there,* it is delivered with a whisper. I know a lie that now disturbs half the kingdom with its noise, which though too proud and great at present to own its parents, I can remember in its whisper-hood. To conclude the nativity of this monster; when it comes into the world without a *sting,* it is still-born; and whenever it loses its sting, it dies.

No wonder, if an infant so miraculous in its birth, should be destined for great adventures: and accordingly we see it has been the guardian spirit of a prevailing party for almost twenty years.

Who can mistake the authorship of "The Art of Political Lying" when he knows *Gulliver's Travels?* What a perfect entryway it is into Houyhnhnm land and the bestial life of the Yahoos! Devils, lies, sins, chains, giants, gods, tumults, seditions, rumours, false reports, rebellion, revenge—all form a characteristic background for the animals who "feed themselves when they are hungry, and bite those that tread upon them." Who but Swift has such constant recourse to monsters?—in this case one "born out of a discarded statesman's head....and *licked* into shape." Who else deals so easily in monsters that scream at the opening of their encasing womb and who die when their sting is lost? Who but Swift the Tory journalist who writes *Gulliver's Travels* during the same years that Defoe creates the characters of Robinson Crusoe and Moll Flanders.

11

II

In the first two decades of the eighteenth century, Steele, Addison, Defoe, and Swift bring qualities of intellect and style to the periodical essay that are not found in it again until the fifties and sixties. In an age which values conversation and the easy style, one natural mode of expression is journal publication. Good conversation provides an inexhaustible fund for periodical literature to draw upon, but great conversation requires great men. Not until mid-century does a peerless talker appear to give new life to the journalism of his time.

Samuel Johnson is himself one of the monuments of English literature. This is very different, for example, from making the same statement about Swift; when we think of Swift we think of his works, while what we remember most about Johnson is his person. Nor is this meant to disparage Johnson's works. If we knew him only through his best and longest poem, "The Vanity of Human Wishes;" the periodical, written almost entirely by himself, *The Rambler;* his great *Dictionary of the English Language;* the incomparable "Idler" essays in *The Universal Chronicle;* his appealing essay "Rasselas, Prince of Abyssinia;" his edition of Shakespeare; and his last work of size, *The Lives of the Poets*—if we knew him only by his works, we would value him greatly. But because we know him also by Boswell's account of his person and his conversation, we know and value the man most of all.

In 1762, when Johnson was fifty-three years old, he received a lifetime pension of £300 a year from the government. Thirty years of real poverty, of constant return in his voluminous writing to the theme of disappointed human wishes, came to an end. Now Johnson could afford the time to indulge his passion and talent for conversation. In the next year he meets the young Boswell, in the following year "The Club" is founded—Johnson, Reynolds, Burke, and Goldsmith are among its original members; Garrick, Fox, and Boswell are later additions—and Johnson has his biographer and his forum. The results, as we know them, are published by Boswell in 1791 as the *Life of Samuel Johnson,* a record of twenty years of incident and conversation created to be recorded by a man born to be a biographer.

Forty years after Boswell gives Johnson to the world, Macaulay reviews Croker's new edition of Boswell's work. In his review he brings together in one enormous sentence a character and a caricature of Dr. Johnson that remain with us to this day:

> Everything about him, his coat, his wig, his figure, his face, his scrofula, his St. Vitus's dance, his rolling walk, his blinking eye, the outward signs which too clearly marked his approbation of his dinner, his insatiable appetite for fish-sauce, and veal-pie with plums, his inextinguishable thirst for tea, his trick of touching the posts as he walked, his mysterious practice of treasuring up scraps of orange-peel, his morning slumbers, his midnight disputations, his contortions, his mutterings, his gruntings, his puffings, his vigorous, acute, and ready eloquence, his sarcastic wit, his vehemence, his insolence, his fits of tempestuous rage...all are as familiar to us as the objects by which we have been surrounded from childhood.

A student of mine once told me that Ben Jonson and Samuel Johnson became confused identities for her after she read Macaulay's description of Johnson and Jonson's portrait of himself in a high-school English course. The portrait is Jonson's surprisingly poignant poem, "My Picture Left in Scotland." After bravely representing himself as equal to "...the youngest Hee, That sits in shadow of Apollo's tree," Jonson suddenly sees himself too clearly:

Oh, but my conscious feares,
>That flie my thoughts betweene.
>Tell me that she hath seene
My hundreds of gray haires,
>Told seven and fortie yeares.
>>Read so much waiste, as she cannot imbrace
>>My mountaine belly, and my rockie face,
>And all these through her eyes, have stopt her eares.

The grunting, huffing, puffing, acute, eloquent, sarcastic, and vehement Samuel Johnson may indeed perceive his Jonsonian belly and rockie face, for he has a penetrating wit. No better example is to be found in his works than in his *Dictionary of the English Language* (1755), a work of remarkable scholarship and memorable humour. Probably most famous is the definition of *network:* "anything reticulated or decussated, at equal distances, with interstices between the intersections." Most notorious is the definition of *oats:* "A grain, which in England is generally given to horses, but in Scotland supports the people." And perhaps most regretted by Johnson, the king's pensioner, is the definition of *pension:* "In England it is generally understood to mean pay given to a state hireling for treason to his country."

Best known to his own age as writer and editor of periodical literature, Johnson's first publications seem to be essays in the *Birmingham Journal* in the early 1730's. Soon after this (1737) he goes to live in London and writes for Edward Cave's *Gentleman's Magazine*. His range is very wide—biographies, Latin verses, essays, poems ("Friendship, an Ode"), and reports of debates in Parliament. In the latter we see the political Johnson (a thorough Tory, he maintains Whiggery to be a politics of disintegration and the Devil to be the first Whig) who does not report Parliamentary speeches so much as he uses them to discuss contemporary political questions in his own language.

But most of this is hack work, and we do not see Johnson at his best until he begins his own periodical in 1750. Then we have the Johnson of *The Rambler,* that extraordinary serial published twice weekly for two years, almost every number written by Johnson himself. In the rank of early English periodicals, *The Rambler* gives place only to *The Spectator* and perhaps to *The Tatler*. Like them, it is a great personal triumph for its author. Unlike them, it is composed primarily of serious essays, some of which belong amongst the best brief critical works of any century.

Everyone who reads *The Rambler* is likely to have a favorite number. The fourth *Rambler,* published on Saturday, March 31, 1750, is my own favorite amongst all of Johnson's short pieces. One of the essay's most interesting aspects is the half-line quoted at its beginning from Thomas Creech, seventeenth century translator of Lucretius and other classical authors: "And join both profit and delight in one." Creech is restating Sir Phillip Sidney's proposition of a hundred years earlier in the *Defense of Poesy* that the dual end of poetry is to teach and to delight. Sidney in turn owes his views to Aristotle, or at least he thinks he does. What seems to be more accurate is that Sidney, Creech, and Johnson add profit (moral improvement) to Aristotle's far simpler criterion of delight.

Johnson understands himself and his age so well that he aims primarily to improve rather than to pleasure. In his eyes, of course, such a distinction is invidious; in answer to it he would undoubtedly retort, "Sir! No true man can be delighted who is not first profitted." The following brief passages, quoted from *Rambler* number four, embody this moral viewpoint and summarize the didactic purpose of Johnson's work:

> The task of our present writers...requires, together with that learning which is to be gained from books, that experience which can never be attained by solitary diligence, but must arise from general converse and accurate observation of the living world...But the fear of not being approved as just copiers of human manners, is not the most important concern an author of this sort ought to have before him....It is justly considered as the greatest excellency of art, to imitate nature; but it is necessary to distinguish those parts of nature

which are most proper for imitation:...It is therefore not a sufficient vindication of a character that it is drawn as it appears; for many characters ought never to be drawn....In narratives where historical veracity has no place, I cannot discover why there should not be exhibited the most perfect idea of virtue....Vice, for vice is necessary to be shown, should always disgust....virtue is the highest proof of understanding, and the only solid basis of greatness.

The Rambler is Johnson's only singular effort in periodical production. His "Idler" essays, often cited in parallel with *The Rambler,* are actually papers on various subjects written for 103 weekly editions of the *Universal Chronicle and Weekly Gazette* published between 8 April 1758 and 5 April 1760. Known for part of its life as *Payne's Universal Chronicle,* this periodical is remembered now for Johnson's contributions to it. Perhaps his most memorable creation in this series is the character of Dick Minim, "a very small critic," who comes to life in Idler number sixty, published on Saturday, 9 June 1759. Johnson's characterization of Criticism, the "goddess easy of access," introduces his brief biography of Minim:

Criticism is a study by which men grow important and formidable at very small expense. The power of invention has been conferred by nature upon few, and the labour of learning those sciences which may, by mere labour, be obtained, is too great to be willingly endured; but every man can exert such judgment as he has upon the work of others; and he whom nature has made weak, and idleness keeps ignorant, may yet support his vanity by the name of a critic.

I hope it will give comfort to great numbers who are passing through the world in obscurity, when I inform them how easily distinction may be obtained. All the other powers of literature are coy and haughty; they must be long courted, and at last are not always gained; but Criticism is a goddess easy of access, and forward of advance, who will meet the slow, and encourage the timorous; the want of meaning she supplies with words, and the want of spirit she supplies with malignity.

Johnson surely has no one man in mind as he spreads his Minim over two numbers of the Idler's observations. But he includes at least a jot of his friend Tobias Smollett, as disputatious a critic as ever lived. It is the Smollett of *Travels through France and Italy* (1766) who provokes from Laurence Sterne in *A Sentimental Journey* the name and character of Smelfungus: "He set out with the spleen and jaundice; and every object he pass'd by was discolored or distorted....I'll tell it, cried Smelfungus, to the world....You had better tell it, said I, to your physician."

This is the same Tobias Smollett who brings such savage realism to the novel in works like *Roderick Random* (1748), *Peregrine Pickle* (1751), and *Humphrey Clinker* which is published posthumously in 1771, the year that Smollett dies. This is also the Smollett who is jailed in 1759 for a libelous piece in the *Critical Review* which he helps found in 1756, edits, and supports as its most frequent contributor until his health breaks in 1763. And it is no other Smollett than the one Lord Shelburne speaks of to David Hume: "How can I take on me the Patronage of a Person, so notorious for libelling as Dr. Smollett? I should disoblige every one whom he has abus'd."

Smollett is himself a grotesque, and the men he creates are often monstrous. Witness Lismahago in *Humphrey Clinker*:

He would have measured about six feet in height had he stood upright; but he stooped very much; was very narrow in the shoulders, and very thick in the calves of his legs, which were cased in black spatter-dashes. As for his thighs, they were long and slender, like those of a grasshopper; his face was, at least, half a yard in length, brown and shrivelled, with projecting cheekbones, little grey eyes of the greenish hue, a large hook nose, a pointed chin, a mouth from ear to ear, very ill

furnished with teeth, and a high narrow forehead,
well furrowed with wrinkles.

In his preface to *Roderick Random*, Smollett writes that his intention is to promote that "generous indignation which ought to animate the reader against the sordid and vicious disposition of the world." Whatever his intention, Smollett sounds like Swift; monstrosity and bestiality are never far from his imagination and his pen.

No better introduction to the eighteenth century novel in general and Smollett's work in particular is available than Smollett's journalism in the *Critical Review* and in the briefly published *Briton* (1762). For Smollett is always a journalist who is sometimes a novelist. Like a journalist and hack writer, he assimilates all materials to his needs and pads shamelessly. A prime example of his padding is the inclusion within *Peregrine Pickle* of an absolutely irrelevant story called "The Memoirs of a Lady of Quality." It matters less that he did not write it himself than that the "Memoirs" are fifth rate fiction that he was probably paid to spread over one hundred and fifty pages of his own novel.

Perceiving the journalist only partially hidden behind the novelist makes Smollett's last and best novel, *The Expedition of Humphrey Clinker*, easier to appreciate and understand. For large parts of it are motivated by journalism's most powerful thrust—reporting men, things, and events in precise detail. Though Smollett's extraordinary capacity for reporting detail is often an impediment to narrative movement, it is also one of the chief adornments of the book. This brief quotation from one of Matthew Bramble's letters to Dr. Lewis is no more remarkable for its loving attention to minutia than several hundred such passages throughout the book:

> By that time we reached Harrigate, I began to be
> visited by certain rheumatic symptoms. The Scotch
> lawyer, Mr. Micklewhimmen, recommended a hot
> bath of these waters so earnestly, that I was
> overpersuaded to try the experiment.—He had used
> it often with success and always stayed an hour in
> the bath, which was a tub filled with Harrigate

water, heated for the purpose. If I could hardly bear the smell of a single tumbler when cold, you may guess how my nose was regaled by the streams arising from a hot bath of the same fluid. At night, I was conducted into a dark hole on the ground floor, where the tub smoaked and stunk like the pot of Acheron, in one corner, and in another stood a dirty bed provided with thick blankets, in which I was to sweat after coming out of the bath. My heart seemed to die within me when I entered this dismal bagnio, and found my brain assaulted by such insufferable effluvia. I cursed Mickle-whimmen for not considering that my organs were formed on this side of the Tweed; but being ashamed to recoil upon the threshold, I submitted to the process.

After having endured all but real suffocation for above a quarter of an hour in the tub, I was moved to the bed and wrapped in blankets.—There I lay a full hour panting with intolerable heat; but not the least moisture appearing on my skin, I was carried to my own chamber, and passed the night without closing an eye, in such a flutter of spirits as rendered me the most miserable wretch in being. I should certainly have run distracted, if the rarefaction of my blood, occasioned by that Stygian bath, had not burst the vessels, and produced a violent haemorrhage, which, though dreadful and alarming, removed the horrible disquiet.—I lost two pounds of blood, and more, on this occasion; and find myself still weak and languid;

However weak and languid Matthew Bramble may feel, Tobias Smollett apparently shares none of his lassitude. Like Bramble a man of multitudinous ills, Smollett produces so much work in little more than a score of writing years that his labors can only be viewed as colossal. His five novels are not a tenth part of his production during that period. Walter Allen, writing in *The English Novel* (1954), notes that Smollett belongs "to the glorious company of English hack writers who have turned their hands to anything. Verse, drama, travel, political writing, a treatise on mid-wifery, translation...and a history of England in many volumes poured from his pen. His novels had to take their chance with the rest, and both his notion of the novel and his craftman-ship are rudimentary compared with Fielding's."

If Smollett is a gifted journalistic hack who sometimes turns his pen to literature, Fielding is an original literary genius who occasionally turns his pen to journalism. Henry Fielding can claim, amongst other accomplishments, personal responsibility for the Licensing Act of 1737 that brings well over 200 years of government censorship to the English stage. The Act is finally provoked by Fielding's two farces, *Pasquin* (1736) and *The Historical Register for 1736* (1737), both savage satirical attacks on the political corruption of the day. As a result of his attacks on the Walpole ministry, Fielding finds himself at the age of thirty a dramatist without a stage; what the drama loses, the novel gains a hundred times over.

Historians of the English novel identify Fielding as source of the tradition that dominates the novel into the second half of the nineteenth century. This tradition of giving literary expression to the social conscience of the age is also in part the tradition of the responsible journalist, which Fielding is before he embarks upon his career as novelist. But Fielding is more than dramatist, journalist, and novelist; he is also one of the most admirable men of his day. Lady Mary Wortley Montague, his cousin, gives us one side of him in this epitaph:

> I am sorry for H. Fielding's death, not only as I shall read no more of his writings, but I believe he lost more than others, as no man enjoyed life more than he did, though few had less reason to do so, the highest of his preferment being raking in the lowest sinks of vice and misery....His happy con-stitution (even when he had, with great pains, half demolished it) made him forget everything when he was before a venison pastry, or over a flask of champagne, and I am persuaded he has known

more happy moments than any prince upon the earth.

The other side of Fielding lies behind Lady Mary's reference to his highest preferment being "raking in the lowest sinks of vice and misery." Fielding is no debauchee; what she refers to is his appointment and tenure, after being banned the stage and becoming a practicing barrister, as Justice of the Peace for Westminster and Middlesex.

Henry Fielding is not only a great novelist, he is a great magistrate as well. That he will be the first and is the second, is respectively foreshadowed and reflected in *The Champion* (1739-40) and *The Covent Garden Journal* (1752). These are his only ventures into journalism as editor and writer, and they bracket his career as novelist which begins in 1742 with *Joseph Andrews* and ends in 1751 with *Amelia.* A clear and impressive insight into the man's character is contained in these two brief sentences written for *Covent Garden Journal* No. 27: "I do not pretend to say, that the mob have no faults; perhaps they have many. I assert no more than this, that they are in all laudable qualities very greatly superior to those who have hitherto, with much injustice, pretended to look down upon them." One has only to remember the age, and the place of "the mob" in its scheme of values, to appreciate the very real humanity of the author of the greatly humane *History of Tom Jones.*

In the estimation of all who know him well, Fielding seems somehow larger than life. To the extent that a great magistrate can be like a runaway boy, Justice Fielding writes himself into the character of Tom Jones. Both his novel and his person dwarf his peers; by contrast, Oliver Goldsmith, twenty-three years younger than Fielding and also a playwright, novelist, and journalist, seems to be dwarfed by them. Goldsmith, too, writes a piece of himself into his most important character—Dr. Primrose, the Vicar of Wakefield—who is as morally pure as Goldsmith's eternally successful play, *She Stoops to Conquer.* But Horace Walpole would never think to say of Fielding, as he says of Goldsmith, that he is "an idiot, with once or twice a fit of parts."

Coming as it does from a Gothic dilettante passing

judgment upon a Sentimental innocent, Walpole's opinion is less surprising and much less convincing than Johnson's, expressed to Fanny Burney, that *The Vicar of Wakefield* "is very faulty; there is nothing of real life in it, and very little of nature." And yet poor Nolly Goldsmith, characterized by Boswell as an inept blunderer with a touch of genius, does manage to write one of the few eighteenth century English novels still read today, one of the two eighteenth century plays still regularly produced today, and various essays and poems famous both in their own time and ours.

Goldsmith not only rivals Fielding and Johnson in versatility, but he is the only hackwriter of the age to match Smollett for sheer tonnage. One important difference between them is that for each enemy made by Dr. Smelfungus, Goldsmith makes a friend. Between the years 1757 and 1762 he writes for at least ten periodicals of different kinds in addition to writing the eight numbers of *The Bee,* published in October and November of 1759. The parallel to Smollett's *Briton* of 1762-63 is remarkable, for both *Bee* and *Briton* run to between 225 and 250 total pages before quietly expiring.

Through Goldsmith's phenomenal production of histories, lives, and collections surpasses forty volumes in the fifteen years left to him after he turns from less lucrative periodical writing, it is as an essayist that he is best known in his own time. Three collections appear within six years, the last being *Essays by Mr. Goldsmith* (1765) assembled from his writings for magazines and newspapers; the most famous is *The Citizen of the World* (1762), a gathering of his "Chinese Letters" which first appear serially in the magazine *The Public Ledger.*

Goldsmith's "Chinese Letters" are his response to the literary fashion which causes European essayists to pose as foreign travellers, usually Oriental, commenting upon the customs and idiosyncracies of an alien culture. Nowhere else in the canon of his work, with the single possible exception of *The Bee,* can the modern reader obtain so clear a view of the mind and temper that create landmarks of English drama, fiction, and poetry. In its style, subject, and humor, Letter IV, quoted in part here, summarizes not only Oliver

Goldsmith but also a significant part of eighteenth century English literature:

LETTERS FROM A CITIZEN OF THE WORLD

LETTER IV. FROM LIEN CHI ALTANGI,
TO THE CARE OF FIPSIHI, RESIDENT
IN MOSCOW, TO BE FORWARDED BY THE
RUSSIAN CARAVAN TO FUM HOAM, FIRST
PRESIDENT OF THE CEREMONIAL ACADEMY
AT PEKIN, IN CHINA.

The English seem as silent as the Japanese, yet vainer than the inhabitants of Siam. Upon my arrival I attributed that reserve to modesty, which I now find has its origin in pride. Condescend to address them first, and you are sure of their acquaintance; stoop to flattery, and you conciliate their friendship and esteem. They bear hunger, cold, fatigue, and all the miseries of life, without shrinking; danger only calls forth their fortitude; they even exult in calamity; but contempt is what they cannot bear. An Englishman fears contempt more than death; he often flies to death as a refuge from its pressure; and dies when he fancies the world has ceased to esteem him.

Pride seems the source not only of their national vices, but of their national virtues also. An Englishman is taught to love his king as his friend, but to acknowledge no other master than the laws which himself has contributed to enact. He despises those nations, who, that one may be free, are all content to be slaves; who first lift a tyrant into terror, and then shrink under his power as if delegated from heaven. Liberty is echoed in all their assemblies; and thousands might be found ready to offer up their lives for the sound, though perhaps not one of all the number understands its meaning. The lowest mechanic, however, looks upon it as his duty to be a watchful guardian of his country's freedom, and often uses a language that might seem haughty, even in the mouth of the great emperor who traces his ancestry to the moon.

A few days ago, passing by one of their prisons, I could not avoid stopping, in order to listen to a dialogue, which I thought might afford me some entertainment. The conversation was carried on between a debtor, through the grate of his prison, a porter, who had stopped to rest his burthen, and a soldier at the window. The subject was upon a threatened invasion from France, and each seemed extremely anxious to rescue his country from the impending danger. For my part, cried the prisoner, *the greatest of my apprehensions is for our freedom; if the French should conquer, what would become of English liberty? My dear friends, liberty is the Englishman's prerogative; we must preserve that at the expense of our lives; of that the French shall never deprive us. It is not to be expected that men who are slaves themselves would preserve our freedom should they happen to conquer.* "Ay, slaves," cries the porter, "they are all slaves, fit only to carry burthens, every one of them. Before I would stoop to slavery, may this be my poison (and he held the goblet in his hand), may this be my poison—but I would sooner 'list for a soldier."

The soldier, taking the goblet from his friend, with much awe fervently cried out, *It is not so much our liberties as our religion that would suffer by such a change; ay, our religion, my lads. May the devil sink me into flames* (such was the solemnity of his adjuration), *if the French should come over, but our religion would be utterly undone.* So saying, instead of a libation, he applied the goblet to his lips, and confirmed his sentiments with a ceremony of the most persevering devotion.

In short, every man here pretends to be a politician; even the fair sex are sometimes found to mix the severity of national altercation with the

24

blandishments of love, and often become conquerors by more weapons of destruction than their eyes.

This universal passion for politics is gratified by Daily Gazettes, as with us in China. But as in ours the Emperor endeavours to instruct his people, in theirs the people endeavour to instruct the administration. You must not, however, imagine, that they who compile these papers have any actual knowledge of the politics or the government of a state; they only collect their materials from the oracle of some coffee-house, which oracle has himself gathered them the night before from a beau at a gaming-table who has pillaged his knowledge from a great man's porter, who has had his information from the great man's gentleman, who has invented the whole story for his own amusement the night preceding.

If the Daily Gazettes Goldsmith mentions were all written in the handsome style he brings to his "Chinese Letter," he would be first to praise rather than damn them as he does. Goldsmith is one of the last defenders of the great English middle style; that he can still write the wonderfully balanced phrases of the Letter's first paragraph—the two sentences beginning with *Condescend* and ending with *bear*—is a tribute both to the strength of the tradition and the soundness of his ear. Rarely again in any form of English prose will the reader hear such careful sound patterns as *condescend, acquaintance, conciliate;* and *first, flattery, friendship* in the first sentence; or *forth, fortitude;* and *calamity, contempt* in the second. Even more rare in English prose will be the considered length of phrase which places ten, ten, and nine syllables respectively in the concluding three clauses of the second sentence. Rarest of all, perhaps, is the combination of fine prose, good sense, and sweet temper with which Oliver Goldsmith improves the nature of the English periodical.

III

Charles Dickens models Harold Skimpole of *Bleak House* on his sometime friend, Leigh Hunt. Skimpole is no friendly portrait, for Hunt is himself a caricature and Dickens' instincts for humbug penetrate to the selfishness beneath Hunt's childish irresponsibility. But Skimpole seems to be more pointedly and painfully Hunt than Dickens intends; at least he regrets the ill-feeling he has caused, and makes partial amends in an essay published on 16 June 1855 in the same periodical, *Household Words,* in which *Bleak House* and Harold Skimpole first serially appeared.

"By Rail to Parnassus" is the name of Dickens' article (probably written with Henry Morley) and it is an unabashed puff for Hunt's new book, *Stories in Verse; Now First Collected.* After publication of the article, Dickens writes to Hunt that he had "thought of the little notice which has given you (I rejoice most heartily to find) so much pleasure—as the best means that could possibly present themselves of enabling me to express myself publically about you as you would desire. In that better and unmistakable association with you by name, let all end."

Four years later, at the age of 75, Hunt is dead and Dickens—in his newly published periodical, *All the Year Round*—makes final amends in "Leigh Hunt. A Remonstrance" (24 December 1859). Though Dickens makes a public end to Hunt as Skimpole, Hunt's better reputation as critical and familiar essayist has survived for more than a hundred vigorous years.

Hunt's career in periodical publications begins with *The Examiner* (1808) and *The Reflector* (1810), both of which he is editing and writing when he and his brother, John, are sentenced to two years in prison for alledgedly libelling the dissolute Prince Regent. Hunt continues to edit *The Examiner* while in prison, where he is accompanied by his family and books and visited by Thomas Moore, Jeremy Bentham, and Charles Lamb amongst others.

Prison seems, if anything, to have strengthened Hunt rather than broken him. Not only did he continue to champion political liberalism with genuine courage, but his gentle, persistent defiance of repressive authority—nicely symbolized in the flowered wallpaper with which he covers his prison room—places him in the forefront of those who have fought with their pens for religious toleration, greater political equality, and abolition of such inhumane practices as slavery and child labor. It is this same thorough liberalism and stubborn dedication which caused Shelley in 1822 to bring Hunt together with Byron in Italy for purposes of producing the magazine called *The Liberal.*

Both Shelley and Byron were Hunt's old acquaintances. Byron was one of his prison visitors, while he introduced Shelley and Keats to each other as well as to the public in his *Examiner.* Hunt was approaching the height of his journalistic powers when he received Shelley's invitation. From 1819 through 1821 he wrote and conducted *The Indicator,* which contains little of literary importance but much of his exceptionally pleasant style. When Hunt accepted Shelley's invitation, therefore, all signs pointed toward a happy collaboration with Byron and a great future for *The Liberal.*,

The signs were tragically wrong. Hunt has hardly settled his family in Italy when Shelley drowns while sailing in the bay of Spezzia. Shelley's real friendship with both men was the strongest link between them; with Shelley gone, "there was a sense of mistake on both sides." Hunt tells the story from his point of view in *Lord Byron and Some of his Contemporaries* (1828). Nothing that he writes elsewhere more clearly reveals subject, author, and era than the following description:

> When I agreed to go to Italy and join in setting
> up the proposed work, Shelley, who was fond of
> giving his friends appellations, happened to be

talking one day with Lord Byron of the mystification which the name of "Leigh Hunt" would cause the Italians; and passing from one fancy to another, he proposed that they should translate it into Leontius. Lord Byron approved of this conceit, and at Pisa was in the habit of calling me so. I liked it; especially as it seemed a kind of new link with my beloved friend [Shelley], then, alas! no more. I was pleased to be called in Italy, what he would have called me there had he been alive: and the familiarity was welcome to me from Lord Byron's mouth, partly because it pleased himself, partly because it was not of a worldly fashion, and the link with my friend was thus rendered compatible. In fact, had Lord Byron been what I used to think him, he might have called me what he chose; and I should have been as proud to be at his call, as I endeavoured to be pleased. As it was, there was something not unsocial nor even unenjoying in our intercourse, nor was there any appearance of constraint; but, upon the whole, it was not pleasant: it was not cordial. There was a sense of mistake on both sides. However, this came by degrees. At first there was hope, which I tried hard to indulge; and there was always some joking going forward; some melancholy mirth, which a spectator might have taken for pleasure.

Our manner of life was this. Lord Byron, who used to sit up at night, writing Don Juan (which he did under the influence of gin and water), rose late in the morning. He breakfasted; read; lounged about, singing an air, generally out of Rossini, and in a swaggering style, though in a voice at once small and veiled; then took a bath, and was dressed; and coming down-stairs, was heard, still singing, in the courtyard, out of which the garden ascended at the back of the house. The servants at the same time brought out two or three chairs. My study, a little room in a corner, with an orange-tree peeping in at the window, looked upon this court-yard. I was generally at my writing when he came down, and either acknowledged his presence by getting up and saying something from the window, or he called out "Leontius!" and came halting up to the window with some joke, or other challenge to conversation. (Readers of good sense will do me the justice of discerning where any thing is spoken of in a tone of objection, and where it is only brought in as requisite to the truth of the picture.) His dress, as at Monte-Nero, was a nankin jacket, with white waistcoat and trowsers, and a cap, either velvet or linen, with a shade to it. In his hand was a tobacco-box, from which he helped himself like unto a shipman, but for a different purpose; his object being to restrain the pinguifying impulse of hunger. Perhaps also he thought it good for the teeth. We then lounged about, or sat and talked, Madame Guiccioli with her sleek tresses descending after her toilet to join us. The garden was small and square, but plenti-fully stocked with oranges and other shrubs; and being well watered, looked very green and refresh-ing under the Italian sky. The lady generally attracted us up into it, if we had not been there before....

He had a delicate white hand, of which he was proud; and he attracted attention to it by rings. He thought a hand of this description almost the only mark remaining now-a-days of a gentleman; of which it certainly is not, nor of a lady either; though a coarse one implies handiwork. He often appeared holding a handkerchief, upon which his jewelled fingers lay imbedded, as in a picture. He was as fond of fine linen as a quaker; and had the remnant of his hair oiled and trimmed with all the anxiety of a Sardanapalus.

The visible character to which this effeminacy gave rise appears to have indicated itself as early as his travels in the Levant, where the Grand Signior is said to have taken him for a woman in disguise. But he had tastes of a more masculine description. He was fond of swimming to the last, and used to push out to a good distance in the Gulf of Genoa. He was also, as I have before mentioned, a good horseman; and he liked to have a great dog or two about him, which is not a habit observable in timid men....

Amongst other things this passage makes clear, it goes some way toward justifying Dickens' creation of Skimpole. " 'Readers of good sense will do me the justice of discerning' that I, Leigh Hunt, can make use of the occasion to regain (at Lord Byron's expense) some of my self-regard lost during that unhappy Italian venture." It is hardly surprising that publication of Hunt's memoirs of Byron after his death, in response to great public demand for Byroniana, leads Hunt into scarifying debate with Moore, Byron's designated biographer, and costs him many friends.

The Liberal lived through four numbers before the mercurial Byron lost interest. The first issue is built around his famous "Vision of Judgment," the second contains his "Heaven and Earth," and the last has his translation of the opening canto of Pulci's "Morgante Maggiore." Then Byron goes off, eventually to join the Greek insurgents and die of fever at Missolongi in 1824. A forlorn Hunt is left in Italy to support his family as best he can.

Before Hunt reaches England again in 1825 he has met Landor and Hazlitt in Florence and been partially revived by Hazlitt's flattering portrait of him in *The Spirit of the Age* (1825). After returning to London, he soon gravitates back to periodical editorship, especially now that his public visibility is greatly increased by publication of *Lord Byron and Some of his Contemporaries*. In 1828 he edits *The Companion;* from 1830 through 1832 he conducts *The Tatler;* 1834-35 finds him writing and editing *Leigh Hunt's London Journal*. Though he does not himself edit another magazine in the years between the *London Journal* and *Leigh Hunt's Journal* (1850-51), he is so well-regarded as a literary figure that he is one of two poets included in the first number of *Household Words* (30 March 1850) when Dickens has his choice of the literary establishment.

This review of Hunt's career as journalist, encompassing Byron's brief contribution, has been intentionally circular: it both begins and ends with Charles Dickens, by any standard of measurement the most important figure in the history of English periodical literature. Dickens is the Steele-Addison-Johnson of his era. Without him, as without them in their time, periodical literature in the nineteenth century would have been undistinguished and indistinct. Dickens gives it stature and form; in return, it gives him the only forum spacious enough to accommodate his prodigious energy, talent, and ego.

Whatever the reason—his biographers and editors have enjoyed speculating upon it—Charles Dickens could not bear the least infringement (whether realized or imagined) upon his authority as editor of the two most famous magazines published in mid-nineteenth century Britain. Was the unfettered novelist simply incapable of functioning within discipline other than his own? Or did his twenty-six months as first editor of *Bentley's Miscellany,* made memorable and miserable for Dickens by publisher Bentley's habitual interference in editorial matters, so affect young Dickens that he determined never again to "bear the perpetual ill will and heart-burnings" of his publisher's influence, much less his domination? From the omniscient perspective of a hundred years, some of the least likely actions of Dickens' subsequent career can be understood when viewed through the anguish of his relationship with Bentley. Perhaps the most remarkable of these actions comes twenty years after Dickens leaves Bentley "to interfere with the *Miscellany*" unimpeded.

From 30 April to 28 May 1859, Dickens assumes the fantastic burden of editing, writing, and re-writing two entirely separate weekly magazines, while publishing one of the two himself and *at the same time writing A Tale of Two Cities.* Perhaps only Dickens could do it; certainly only Dickens could find reason to do it. His reason is that he must have absolute control of the periodical he edits. To anyone else his control of *Household Words* (1850-59) may appear absolute, but to Dickens all periodical publishers are potential Bentleys. Thus for five remarkable weeks in the spring of 1859, Dickens brings the most successful publication of its time to a close while simultaneously beginning another destined to eclipse every success of its predecessor.

All the Year Round is the name of the new periodical; together with *Household Words,* it constitutes the longest continuous run of distinguished publication under a single editor in the history of English magazines. From March of 1850 through June of 1870 Dickens is the primary source of intellect and energy for weekly periodicals so popular that they ultimately reach the amazing audience of 300,000 purchasing readers. His comment to Leigh Hunt upon *Household Words* could be made about either publication at almost any time during his twenty years of stewardship: It is, he writes, "a great humming-top...always going round with the weeks, and murmuring 'Attend to me.'" Attend to it he does, raising both *Household Words* and *All the Year Round* to a level never before or since attained by English periodical publication.

Unlike Tobias Smollett, whose picaresque novels please him and whose exaggerated characters instruct him, Dickens is entirely a journalist whose work cannot be understood without reference to its journalistic background. It is altogether appropriate that Dickens' first published story should appear in 1833 in the *Monthly Magazine* and his last completed work should be printed in *All the Year Round.* Though the former was collected into *Sketches by Boz* (1836) and the latter included in the 1866 edition of *The Uncommercial Traveller,* both are occasional sketches whose style and subject are shaped to the periodicals which publish them.

Just as this is true for his occasional pieces, so is it true for Dickens' novels. All fourteen are published either in weekly or monthly parts, six of them—*Oliver Twist, The Old Curiosity Shop, Barnaby Rudge, Hard Times, A Tale of Two Cities,* and *Great Expectations* — as serial features in four different magazines. Edgar Johnson evokes contemporary

"Familiar in their Mouths as HOUSEHOLD WORDS."—Shakespeare.

HOUSEHOLD WORDS.

𝔄 𝔚𝔢𝔢𝔨𝔩𝔶 𝔍𝔬𝔲𝔯𝔫𝔞𝔩.

CONDUCTED BY

CHARLES DICKENS.

VOLUME V.

FROM THE 20TH OF MARCH TO THE 11TH OF SEPTEMBER.

Being from No. 104 to No. 129.

LONDON:
OFFICE, 16, WELLINGTON STREET NORTH.
1852.

public reaction to Dickens' novels in his introduction to the Washington Square Press edition of *Oliver Twist:*

For the greater part of 1837 almost everyone who could read in England was enthusiastically gulping down two novels appearing simultaneously in monthly installments. (And a good many who couldn't read, assembled in excited groups, were having them read aloud.) Both were by a brilliant young novelist of twenty-five who had just burst upon the world. The opening number of the earlier of the two had made its bow in April of the preceding year as a modest green-paper-covered pamphlet, and for the three following numbers had seemed a failure. The few reviewers who noticed it at all dismissed it as a "dull" and "enigmatic" effort to exploit a vein of "exhausted comicality," and probably not more than five hundred out of the fifteen hundred copies printed were sold.

Then, suddenly, it caught on. Back numbers had to be printed in mounting quantities; before the end, forty thousand copies of each issue were being devoured. All England was wild about *Pickwick Papers* and Charles Dickens was famous. His plump and amiable little hero with his gaiters and benevolently gleaming spectacles, together with Sam Weller, his cockney squire, and all the other thronging characters in the story, had become more than national figures: they were a mania. People named their pets after Isabella Wardle and Mr. Winkle; there were Pickwick chintzes, Pickwick cigars, Pickwick hats, canes, and coats; Weller corduroys, Boz cabs, not to mention countless plagiarisms, parodies, and sequels, in print and on the stage. While Pickwick still had nine months to run, *Oliver Twist* began in *Bentley's Miscellany,* and almost at once scaled hardly less delirious heights of popularity.

The Posthumous Papers of the Pickwick Club, the seldom-used full title of *The Pickwick Papers,* itself suggests one of the most significant facts in Dickens' biography. While a boy in the English town of Chatham, he not only reads all he can find of Swift, Fielding, Smollett, and Defoe, but he also reads Addison and Steele's *Tatler,* their *Spectator,* Johnson's *Idler,* and Goldsmith's *Citizen of the World.* In his mature years he still gratefully remembers the gift of Goldsmith's collected *Bee* given him by his Chatham schoolmaster, William Giles, as a parting present on the occasion of his family's permanent removal to London.

This extensive childhood reading in the best and earliest of English periodicals greatly influences Dickens in his later notions of what a magazine should be. Writing to Giles in 1848, a quarter-century after leaving Chatham, Dickens' language reflects his debt to Goldsmith when he refers to his own work as "fledging...little Bees...whose humming has been heard abroad." More important than metaphor, however, is the legacy of form that Dickens inherits from his reading of early periodicals.

The Pickwick Papers clearly reflects this legacy. It takes what form it has from the convention of the Club, modelled after Steele and Addison's Spectator Club. In Dickens' version, Samuel Pickwick is general chairman of the Club which bears his name; together with members Tupman, Snodgrass, and Winkle, he forms a Corresponding Society which is charged with reporting its members' journeys and adventures, including their observations upon men's actions and manners, to the larger membership of the Club.

Dickens is no more successful than Steele and Addison in giving life to all his characters. Just as Mr. Spectator becomes the composite personality of his clubmates, so does Mr. Pickwick become the life of his Society. The book is episodic, anecdotal, formless—and wildly successful. Perhaps its success is too great for young Dickens to perceive that it succeeds in spite of the Pickwick Club, for the pattern of the Club is still strong in his imagination when he writes in 1839 to John Forster, his friend and later his biographer, of his idea for a new weekly periodical:

The best general idea of the plan of the work

might be given perhaps by reference to *The Tatler, The Spectator,* and Goldsmith's *Bee.* I should propose to start as *The Spectator* does, with some pleasant fiction relative to the origin of the publication; to introduce a little club or knot of characters and to carry their personal histories and proceedings through the work; to introduce fresh characters constantly; to reintroduce Mr. Pickwick and Sam Weller, the latter of whom might furnish an occasional communication with great effect; to write essays on the various foibles of the day as they arise; to take advantage of all passing events; and to vary the form of the papers by throwing into them sketches, essays, tales, adventures, letters from imaginary correspondents and so forth, so as to diversify the contents as much as possible.

I would also commence and continue from time to time, a series of satirical papers purporting to be translated from some Savage Chronicles, and to describe the administration of justice in some country that never existed, and record the proceedings of its wise men. The object of this series (which if I can compare it with anything would be something between *Gulliver's Travels* and the Citizen of the World) would be to keep a special look-out upon the magistrates in town and country, and never to leave those worthies alone.

Dickens writes this to Forster in July of 1839. In October he brings out the first number of *Master Humphrey's Clock,* the only unsuccessful periodical with which he is ever associated. Its failure is as remarkable as the popularity of its successors. Dickens' name is by now sufficient to guarantee large early sales, but his name alone is not enough to hold the thousands of expectant readers who spend their pennies to buy a serialized novel and discover that they have purchased instead an old-fashioned periodical.

When sales begin to reflect the public's disappointment, Dickens makes great alterations in *Master Humphrey's Clock.* Rapidly dispensing with essay-forms imported from the

Spectator and *Idler*, he turns his attention to fiction, changing the shape of *The Old Curiosity Shop* from a first-person short story narrated by Master Humphrey to a third-person novel which relentlessly carries Little Nell, her grandfather, and the monstrous Quilp into an impassable swamp of pathos.

As for the clock itself, Dickens guts it, leaving only the case intact in order to display *The Old Curiosity Shop* and, later, *Barnaby Rudge.* Dickens learns part of his lesson well, but it is a lesson whose full meaning he cannot yet comprehend. Following the breakdown of the *Clock,* he has a brief, unhappy association with the *Daily News*—a journal which he founds in 1846 and edits for less than three weeks, parting from it after recurrent clashes with Bradbury the publisher—and writes a series of five Christmas Books from 1843 through 1847 (*A Christmas Carol,* 1843, is best known) as well as *Dombey and Son* in 1848 and *David Copperfield* in 1849-50.

But periodical publication is never far from Dickens' mind; as early as November of 1846 he writes to Forster his thoughts about another weekly magazine: "As to the Review, I strongly incline to the notion of a kind of Spectator (Addison's)—very cheap, and pretty frequent." Three years, two Christmas books, and two novels later, he is still pursuing the same subject and Mr. Spectator is still with him. This time he writes to Forster of his desire to establish in the periodical he is planning "a certain SHADOW....a creature which isn't the Spectator and isn't Isaac Bickerstaff...but in which people will be perfectly willing to believe, and which is just as mysterious and quaint enough to have a sort of charm for their imagination, while it will represent common-sense and humanity."

Fortunately for both Dickens and *Household Words,* which is less than six months from reality, Forster is not in the thrall of Chatham memories. He thinks the plan impracticable and says so. The Shadow-Spectator is finally dropped, not to appear again until Dickens has demonstrated his absolute mastery of periodical form and audience in both *Household Words* and *All the Year Round.* When next the ghost of Addison's Spectator is evoked by Dicken's pen, he is the justly famous Uncommercial Traveller who works for "the great house of Human Interest Brothers," travelling city streets and country roads, "seeing many little things and some great things, which, because they interest me, I think may interest others."

Amongst Dickens' interests are titles. He agonizes over the choice of a name for his new venture: *Mankind? Everything? Charles Dickens?* (Whatever his problems, at least his ego is sufficient.) When he finally strikes upon *Household Words,* he thinks it "a very pretty name." In the first number, published under the date of 30 March 1850, Dickens tells his readers that the new magazine has but a single goal—"to live in the Household affections, and to be numbered among the Household thoughts of our readers." Which it does, and is, for more than nine exceptional years.

Dickens is undeniably the soul of its success. But he is far too experienced by this time to rely upon himself alone. Not only is he blessed with the perfect alter-ego in his sub-editor, Henry Wills, but his taste in contributing writers is extraordinary: Wilkie Collins, Mrs. Gaskell, George Meredith, Elizabeth Barrett Browning, Leigh Hunt, Walter Savage Landor, Bulwer Lytton, Coventry Patmore—all grace the pages of *Household Words,* whether writing for it on salary (Collins), frequently (Meredith), or only as occasionally as Mrs. Browning.

Imaginary literature is not Dickens' only aim for his new magazine. He writes to Michael Faraday, the great British experimental physicist whose discovery of electro-magnetic induction made possible both the modern dynamo and electric motor, asking him for a novel sort of contribution: "It has occurred to me that it would be extremely beneficial to a large class of the public to have some account of your late lectures on the breakfast-table, and of those you addressed last year to children. I should be extremely glad to have some papers in reference to them, published in my new enterprise *Household Words.*" Faraday sends his lecture notes which are reworked and published in the late summer and autumn of 1850 as "The Chemistry of a Candle," "The

Laboratory in the Chest," and "The Mysteries of a Tea-Kettle."

The first and only crisis for Dickens' magazine occurs during the winter of 1853-54. Its genesis is speculative, but the vantage point of a full century gives an interesting view: From March through November of 1850 Dickens is not only editor of *Household Words* and its single largest contributor, he is also author of the last nine monthly pamphlets of *David Copperfield*. A year later he is supplying his public with the monthly parts of *Bleak House,* which does not conclude until well into 1853. Like *David Copperfield, Bleak House* is published apart from the pages of *Household Words.* Its twentieth and final monthly number coincides remarkably with the onset of crisis in the circulation of Dickens' magazine.

Are the two circumstances connected beyond coincidence? Do Dickens' readers buy his weekly magazine because they are moved by their profound engagement with his monthly-pamphlet novels to read all that comes from his hand? Dickens seems to think so; for remedy of *Household Words'* falling sickness he turns to himself and expands the pages of the magazine with weekly installments of a new novel, *Hard Times,* throughout 1854 and 1855. The first portion appears on 1 April 1854. Ten weeks later circulation has doubled and *Household Words* is never in trouble again.

This time Dickens absorbs fully the lesson he began to learn with the unwinding of *Master Humphrey's Clock.* He may view himself as successor and inheritor of Steele-Addison, Johnson, and Goldsmith; of Mr. Spectator, Isaac Bickerstaff, and the Citizen of the World. History will fully vindicate his opinion. But he must not confuse his view of himself with the author perceived and valued by a large part of his reading public. What they see is Dickens-the-novelist, the premier writer of English fiction in his time; what they expect is a flood of memorable stories and powerful characters created solely to engage them in adventures more moving than their own lives provide.

Never again does the journalist forget to give the public what it expects of the novelist. The opening number of *All the Year Round* contains the first part of *The Tale of Two Cities,* and every subsequent issue contains a weekly installment until the novel is finished. Soon after its conclusion, Dickens is writing *Great Expectations,* again solely for distribution through the pages of *All the Year Round.* In the space between *Hard Times* and *The Tale of Two Cities,* when *Household Words* is that "great humming-top" with a life of its own, Dickens feels safe in committing *Little Dorrit* to monthly pamphlets. When *All the Year Round* is at the peak of its success, following massive infusion of strength from *The Tale of Two Cities* and *Great Expectations,* Dickens again allows himself the (largely financial) liberty of pamphlet publication for a novel—this time *Our Mutual Friend.*

Much that is true and significant has been written about the influence of periodic publication upon Dickens' novels. Whether serially printed in magazine or pamphlet form, the effects of divided publication are predictable and apparent. Readers often remark the episodic arrangement of Dickens' material, with each section ending in an enticement to the buyer of tuppeny numbers or shilling pamphlets to return for at least one more episode. The same motivation may also account for the enormous length of most of the novels: when eighteen-to-twenty monthly pamphlets or eighty weekly numbers are required, then 400,000 words is not too many to fulfill the demand.

Length, rhythm, and cohesion are not the only aspects of the novel likely to be affected, though they are three dimensions of the narrative most susceptible to requirements of periodic publication. A second group is composed of subject selection, nature and number of characters, and choice of language. These three are likely to be influenced only to the extent of the author's committment to and comprehension of the form within which he works. For Dickens, with his unreserved committment, and his unequalled understanding of periodic publication—subject, character, and language are no less affected than length, rhythm, and cohesion.

Though any of the novels might serve to illustrate Dickens' accommodation to his medium, I have chosen *Bleak House* because Dickens writes it at the peak of his accomplishment and because it seems to me the most Dickensian of novels. Its sixty-seven chapters and 400,000 words encompass as rich a selection of character and action as writer can offer and reader can bear. Published in 1852 and 1853 in twenty monthly numbers of approximately 20,000 words each, *Bleak House* is cut to the pattern of previous successes such as *David Copperfield* and *Oliver Twist*. Its twenty installments, each divided into three or four chapters, are at once self-contained stories and open invitations to the next section. The closing paragraphs of the first six installments give a fair idea of Dickens' practice throughout the book:

I End of Chapter Four

The purblind day was feebly struggling with the fog, when I opened my eyes to encounter those of a dirty-faced little spectre fixed upon me. Peepy had scaled his crib, and crept down in his bedgown and cap, and was so cold that his teeth were chattering as if he had cut them all.

II End of Chapter Seven

The housekeeper has dropped her voice to little more than a whisper.

"She had been a lady of a handsome figure and a noble carriage. She never complained of the change; she never spoke to any one of being crippled, or of being in pain; but, day by day, she tried to walk upon the terrace; and, with the help of a stick, and with the help of the stone balustrade, went up and down, up and down, up and down, in sun and shadow, with greater difficulty every day. At last, one afternoon, her husband (to whom she had never, on any persuasion, opened her lips since that night), standing at the great south window, saw her drop upon the pavement. He hastened down to raise her, but she repulsed him as he bent over her, and looking at him fixedly and coldly, said, 'I will die here, where I have walked. And I will walk here, though I am in my grave. I will walk here, until the pride of this house is humbled. And when calamity, or when disgrace is coming to it, let the Dedlocks listen for my step!"....."There and then she died. And from those days," says Mrs. Rouncewell, "the name has come down—The Ghost's Walk. If the tread is an echo, it is an echo that is only heard after dark, and is often unheard for a long while together. But it comes .back, from time to time; and so sure as there is sickness or death in the family, it will be heard then."...."That is the story. Whatever the sound is, it is a worrying sound," says Mrs. Rouncewell, getting up from her chair, "and what is to be noticed in it, is, that it *must be heard*. My Lady, who is afraid of nothing, admits that when it is there, it must be heard."...."Now, come hither," says the housekeeper. "Hither, child, towards my Lady's pillow. I am not sure that it is dark enough yet, but listen! Can you hear the sound upon the terrace, through the music, and the beat [of the clock] and everything?" "I certainly can!" "So my Lady says."

III End of Chapter Ten

For, on a low bed opposite the fire, a confusion of dirty patchwork, lean-ribbed ticking, and coarse sacking, the lawyer, hesitating just within the doorway, sees a man. He lies there, dressed in shirt and trousers, with bare feet. He has a yellow look, in the spectral darkness of a candle that has guttered down, until the whole length of its wick (still burning) had doubled over, and left a tower of winding-sheet above it. His hair is ragged, mingling with his whiskers and his beard—the latter, ragged too, and grown, like the scum and

41

mist around him, in neglect. Foul and filthy as the room is, foul and filthy as the air, it is not easy to perceive what fumes those are which most oppress the senses in it; but through the general sickliness and faintness, and the odour of stale tobacco, there comes into the lawyer's mouth the bitter, vapid taste of opium.

"Hallo, my friend!" he cries, and strikes his iron candlestick against the door.

He thinks he has awakened his friend. He lies a little turned away, but his eyes are surely open.

"Hallo, my friend!" he cries again. "Hallo! Hallo!"

As he rattles on the door, the candle which has drooped so long, goes out, and leaves him in the dark; with the gaunt eyes in the shutters staring down upon the bed.

IV End of Chapter Thirteen

I have omitted to mention in its place, that there was some one else at the family dinner party. It was not a lady. It was a gentleman. It was a gentleman of a dark complexion—a young surgeon. He was rather reserved, but I thought him very sensible and agreeable. At least, Ada asked me if I did not, and I said yes.

V End of Chapter Sixteen

Sir Leicester is fidgety, down at Chesney Wold, with no better company than the gout; he complains to Mrs. Rouncewell that the rain makes such a monotonous pattering on the terrace, that he can't read the paper, even by the fireside in his own snug dressing-room.

"Sir Leicester would have done better to try the other side of the house, my dear," says Mrs. Rouncewell to Rosa. "His dressing-room is on my Lady's side. And in all these years I never heard the

step upon the Ghost's Walk, more distinct than it is
to-night!'"

VI End of Chapter Nineteen

Jo moves on, through the long vacation, down to
Blackfriars Bridge, where he i..nds a baking stony
corner wherein to settle to his repast.

And there he sits, munching and gnawing, and
looking up at the great Cross on the sur ımit of St.
Paul's Cathedral, glittering above a red and violet-
tinted cloud of smoke. From the boy's face one
might suppose that sacred emblem to be, in his
eyes, the crowning confusion of the great, confused city; so golden, so high up, so far out of his
reach. There he sits, the sun going down, the river
running past, the crowd flowing by him in two
streams—everything moving on to some purpose
and to one end—until he is stirred up, and told to
"move on" too.

In six brief, strategically placed passages, Dickens rings and
echoes thematic change on his *Bleak House* bells. At the
conclusion of installments one and six he has evoked the
pathos which is never far from his emotions when he
considers the lot of mistreated children. Sections two and
five end with the fearful forewarning of the unquiet ghost,
while three and four offer the powerful contrast of the
hopeless degradation and death of a man disgraced, and the
hopeful, happy promise of a sensible young man perceived
through the eyes of a saintly young woman.

Not only do the six endings represent the episodic
structure of the book, but they also represent a typical
configuration in Dickens' narrative practice. Sections three
and four conclude with examples of hope and despair, while
sections one-two and five-six form parallel borders of pathos
and foreboding. Whether living in the shadows of the
pathetic, fearful periphery or in the alternately cold and
warm light of the center, Dickens' characters move to the
measured beat and relentless demand of periodic publication.

This demand dictates not only length and the rhythm of configuration, but coherence as well. By coherence I mean both the fitting together of parts and the justification of individual passages. This justification is bound to be different as demands of form differ. In the case of magazine and pamphlet publication, variety and extent inevitably prevail over tightness of fit. No brief passage in all of Dickens' writing seems to me better to illustrate this principle than the opening four paragraphs of chapter sixteen in *Bleak House:*

My Lady Dedlock is restless, very restless. The astonished fashionable intelligence hardly knows where to have her. To-day, she is at Chesney Wold; yesterday, she was at her house in town; to-morrow, she may be abroad, for anything the fashionable intelligence can with confidence predict. Even Sir Leicester's gallantry has some trouble to keep pace with her. It would have more, but that his other faithful ally, for better and for worse—the gout—darts into the old oak bed-chamber at Chesney Wold, and grips him by both legs.

Sir Leicester receives the gout as a trouble-some demon, but still a demon of the patrician order. All the Dedlocks, in the direct male line, through a course of time during and beyond which the memory of man goeth not to the contrary, have had the gout. It can be proved, sir. Other men's fathers may have died of the rheumatism, or may have taken base contagion from the tainted blood of the sick vulgar; but the Dedlock family have communciated something exclusive, even to the levelling process of dying, by dying of their own family gout. It has come down, through the illustrious line, like the plate, or the pictures, or the place in Lincolnshire. It is among their dignities. Sir Leicester is, perhaps, not wholly without an impression, though he has never resolved it into words, that the angel of death in the discharge of his necessary duties may observe to the shades of the aristocracy, "My lords and gentlemen, I have the honour to present to you another Dedlock certified to have arrived per the family gout."

Hence, Sir Leicester yields up his family legs to the family disorder, as if he held his name and fortune on that feudal tenure. He feels, that for a Dedlock to be laid upon his back and spasmodically twitched and stabbed in his extremities, is a liberty taken somewhere; but, he thinks, "We have all yielded to this; it belongs to us; it has, for some hundreds of years, been understood that we are not to make the vaults in the park interesting on more ignoble terms; and I submit myself to the compromise."

And a goodly show he makes, lying in a flush of crimson and gold, in the midst of the great drawing-room, before his favourite picture of my Lady, with broad strips of sunlight shining in, down the long perspective, through the long line of windows, and alternating with soft reliefs of shadow. Outside, the stately oaks, rooted for ages in the green ground which has never known ploughshare, but was still a Chase when kings rode to battle with sword and shield, and rode a hunting with bow and arrow; bear witness to his greatness. Inside, his forefathers, looking on him from the walls, say, "Each of us was a passing reality here, and left this coloured shadow of himself, and melted into remembrance as dreamy as the distant voices of the rooks now lulling you to rest;" and bear their testimony to his greatness, too. And he is very great this day. And woe to Boythorn, or other daring wight, who shall presumptuously contest an inch with him!

Lady Dedlock's restlessness is important to the story; Lord Dedlock's gout is important only to Lord Dedlock. But it does give Dickens opportunity for a five-hundred word digression, which can be very welcome when an author's imagination is put to the monthly strain of producing 20,000 publishable words for twenty consecutive months.

Bleak House is over-long, it rises to peaks which are distractingly rhythmic in their periodic occurrence, and a good many of its parts do not fill significant places in the whole. Having said that, however, one has said surprisingly little about the quality of the novel. The plain fact is that *Bleak House* pays a price for periodic publication that is miniscule when compared to the benefits it receives. In matters of subject, language, and character it is the beneficiary of incomparable advantage, for Dickens writes to a model whose requirements exactly fit the measure of his extraordinary talent.

Unlike most of his fellow novelists in mid-nineteenth century Britain, Dickens does not choose his subjects by viewing the world through the tinted glasses of romance. He does not, for example, believe industrial propaganda which promises to produce both goods and machinery capable of raising the poor and revitalizing the nation. After years of poverty in London, including apprenticing in a warehouse and witnessing his father's imprisonment for debt, Dickens has no illusions about either poverty or industry. After years of working as a court reporter, he cannot follow Bulwer and Ainsworth in idealizing criminals nor can he rationalize the vicious acts committed in the name of justice by venal lawyers and judges. The subject of *Bleak House*—the endless Chancery Court suit of Jarndyce and Jarndyce joined with the sin of Lady Dedlock, the evil of Lawyer Tulkinghorn, and their individual retributions—rises directly from this experience and takes its shape from Dickens' reportorial conviction that serious writing should be directed toward social reform.

Bleak House is typical of Dickens' novels in its choice of subject. Having felt the personal anguish of class inferiority, having lived and worked amongst the damaged, exploited, and depraved of his society, Dickens is never so convincing (if never so extreme) as when he is reporting scenes in the workhouse or Fleet Prison, in a dreadful school like Dotheboys Hall or an equally dreadful city like Coketown.

Titles like *Bleak House* and *Hard Times* share the influence of reportorial point with names like Chuzzlewit, Quilp, Stiggins, Swiveller, and Wackford Squeers. Writing in *A Literary History of England,* Samuel Chew identifies Dickens' practice in these terms:

> Dickens does not look beneath the surface....His is essentially a grotesque art, the art of the caricaturist, even when the result is not, properly speaking, caricature. But though to secure an effect a weakness is overemphasized, there is unerring insight in detecting the weakness. He sees the outward man rather than the inward motive; there is little effort to trace the development of character; and when once the idiosyncracy or "humor" is established, the person either remains what he is to the end of the story or else undergoes a violent and unconvincing change at the close for the sake of the plot. A disconcerting feature of Dickens' work is the juxtaposition of the fantastic and the real. Creatures who live only in his imagination, though there with unexampled vitality, jostle with people drawn from actuality. Similarly, melodramatic incident protrudes with startling suddenness from a context which is real.

Chew is right, so far as he goes. But he does not go far enough. Dickens' art is grotesque; he is indeed a caricaturist; and the result, properly speaking, is neither caricature nor grotesquerie. It is neither because it is chiefly reportorial: that is, it depends far more upon description than upon explanation. Its brilliance lies in the sense it conveys of absolute fidelity to surfaces, that same fidelity which causes such a stir in the 1830's when it shapes itself into the characters of *Pickwick* and *Oliver Twist;* that same fidelity, a quarter-century later, which takes *Household Words* and *All the Year Round* to unprecedented success.

Chew is also right about the remarkable—he calls it "disconcerting"—juxtaposition of reality and fantasy in Dickens' characters. Imaginary creatures and real people stand together as though Dickens had little sense of their essential incongruity. What Chew does not say, however, is that incongruity is a function of the need for reconciliation. Feeling no such need, Dickens describes what he sees and leaves the problem of explanation to those for whom surfaces are merely impediments to analysis.

Dickens' choice of subject and portrayal of character both profit greatly from his reportorial view and commitment to periodic publication. So also does his language. Just as the reader should expect Dickens' mode of publication to affect most adversely the coherence and rhythm of his novels, so should he expect the happiest effect to be seen in Dickens' characters and language. It is, therefore, no surprise to discover that the immense breadth and variety of polished surface reflected by his characters has its rhetorical counterpart in his greatly heightened language.

I have chosen the following two paragraphs from the beginning of chapter twenty-five in *Bleak House* because they seem to me to be as unremarkable in their context as they are exemplary in their content:

There is disquietude in Cook's Court, Cursitor Street. Black suspicion hides in that peaceful region. The mass of Cook's Courtiers are in their usual state of mind, no better and no worse; but, Mr. Snagsby is changed, and his little woman knows it.

For, Tom-All-Alone's and Lincoln's Inn Fields persist in harnessing themselves, a pair of ungovernable coursers, to the chariot of Mr. Snagsby's imagination; and Mr. Bucket drives; and the passengers are Jo and Mr. Tulkinghorn; and the complete equipage whirls through the Law Stationery business at wild speed, all around the clock. Even in the little front kitchen where the family meals are taken, it rattles away at a smoking pace from the dinner table, when Mr. Snagsby pauses in carving the first slice of the leg of mutton baked with potatoes, and stares at the kitchen wall.

In less than one hundred and fifty words Dickens manages a rich rhetorical example of "the juxtaposition of the fantastic and the real" which Chew finds so disconcerting when it is exemplified in character. Tom-All-Alone's and Lincoln's Inn Fields—two utterly different sections of nineteenth century London—are no more unlikely a matched pair than Jo the cornersweeper and Lawyer Tulkinghorn or the vision before Snagsby's eyes and the homely scene in the kitchen at Cook's Court. But Dickens no more than any other experienced reporter and magazine writer limits his search for heightened impact to the coupling of disparate images. His most natural recourse and powerful ally is heightened language, which he uses always with effect if sometimes without mercy:

In so brief a passage, *disquietude* reigns. *Suspicion* is *black,* the *coursers ungovernable,* their *speed wild,* and their *pace* no less than *smoking.* The *equipage* not only *whirls,* it *rattles.* Through it all, *Snagsby* himself *stares.* By necessary contrast, the *peaceful region* surrounding Snagsby is filled by the *usual mass* of Cook's Courtiers, especially his *little woman* in his *little front-kitchen.*

Bleak House supplies such passages almost too frequent to number. The first paragraph of the very next chapter, number twenty-six, exemplifies the expansive catagorizing and listing which are so much a part of Dickens' rhetoric:

Wintry morning, looking with dull eyes and sallow face upon the neighborhood of Leicester Square, finds its inhabitants unwilling to get out of bed. Many of them are not early risers at the brightest of times, being birds of night who roost when the sun is high, and are wide awake and keen for prey when the stars shine out. Behind dingy blind and curtain, in upper story and garret, skulking more or less under false names, false hair, false titles, false jewellry, and false histories, a colony of brigands lie in their first sleep. Gentlemen of the green baize road who could discourse, from personal experience, of foreign gallups and home treadmills; spies of strong governments who eternally quake with weakness and miserable fear, broken traitors, cowards, bullies, gamesters, shuf-

flers, swindlers, and false witnesses; some not
unmarked by the branding-iron, beneath their dirty
braid; all with more cruelty in them than was in
Nero, and more crime than is in Newgate.

A surface art? Perhaps. But these are surfaces shaped by
the heat of an imagination unequalled in its variety and
fecundity, an imagination tuned to its full stretch upon the
sounding board of periodical literature. Neither Charles
Dickens nor the English novel can be fully enjoyed or
understood without reference to periodicals like *Household
Words* and *All the Year Round.*

.

IV

Where Steele and Addison create a new literary species, Dickens creates a new audience for literature. Once having created an audience, he proceeds to re-create them in his own image (no great task for a man who sees equivalence amongst periodical titles like *Mankind, Everything,* and *Charles Dickens*), then bequeath them to his contemporaries and successors. Most important of these sometimes unwilling heirs are Anthony Trollope and William Makepeace Thackeray.

Thackeray's career lies in remarkable chronological parallel to Dickens'. The decade of the thirties sees both of them enter public literary life for the first time. Eighteen thirty-two is a temporal watershed: Scott's last novel, *Castle Dangerous;* his death; Lord John Russell's monumental Reform Bill—all precede, and in a sense each prepares for, the entrance of Dickens and Thackeray. In the brief period from 1833 to 1835, Dickens is first published in the *Monthly Magazine* and Thackeray has his earliest pieces in *Fraser's Magazine.* During the last four years of the decade, both are publishing their first three novel-length works. While Dickens produces *Pickwick, Oliver Twist,* and *Nicholas Nickelby,* Thackeray is busy with *The Yellowplush Correspondence, Major Gahagan,* and *Catherine.* To extend the coincidence, *Major Gahagan* is offered serially by the *New Monthly Magazine* while the other two are published periodically in *Fraser's.*

Unfortunately for Thackeray, to this point his career parallels Dickens' only in time. His first three novels are as much forgotten as Dickens' are remembered, and his work

51

during the early and mid-forties is equally undistinguished. While Dickens is establishing himself with a major run of novels and Christmas books, Thackeray is writing in a minor key. His best effort during this period is published in *Punch,* for which he is a staff writer from 1842 through 1848, under the title *The Snobs of England. By One of Themselves* (later better known as *The Book of Snobs*). But it is not until 1847-48 that Thackeray finds his natural mode and becomes famous: *Vanity Fair* appears in twenty monthly numbers while Dickens is preparing *David Copperfield.* The pamphlet-buying public has seldom been able to purchase so much for its shilling as it could during those wonderful months from 1847 through 1850.

Though both authors reach a creative peak in mid-century, Thackeray does not again approach the level of *Vanity Fair* while Dickens still has *Bleak House* and *Great Expectations* ahead of him. Like Dickens, from whose example he profits, Thackeray makes two trips to America to give public readings. During this same period he writes for serial publication three popular novels —*Pendennis, Henry Esmond, The Newcomes*—and one less well received. Again like Dickens he bases this unsuccessful novel on his American voyages: *The Virginians* is no more successful than *Martin Chuzzlewit,* both showing the strain of scene-shifting between familiar England and alien America.

The Thackeray-Dickens parallel has one more significant stage. In 1859,the year Dickens begins *All the Year Round*, Thackeray completes periodic publication of *The Virginians* and becomes editor of the new *Cornhill Magazine.* To give his magazine the most hopeful beginning, Dickens wisely calls upon himself for *A Tale of Two Cities* closely followed by *Great Expectations.* Equally wise as an editor, Thackeray calls upon the other most successful novelist of the time to fill *Cornhill's* competing pages: Anthony Trollope writes the fourth of his Barchester novels, *Framley Parsonage,* for the opening numbers of Thackeray's magazine.

Though Thackeray resigns the editorship when he finds the responsibility oppressive, he follows Trollope in *Cornhill's* pages with his last two complete novels and, posthumously, with an unfinished third: *Lovel the Widower, The Adventures of Phillip,* and a fragment called *Denis Duval. Cornhill* profits from their presence, even if they make clear Thackeray's good judgment in selecting Trollope to do battle with Dickens in the early competition for readers.

Trollope repays Thackeray's faith in him, for Thackeray happily admits that *Framley Parsonage* is responsible for *Cornhill Magazine's* immediate success. Though only four years his junior, Trollope regards Thackeray as master and model—to the point that he imitates *Vanity Fair* in one of his unsuccessful later novels (*The Way We Live Now,* 1875) and in 1879 writes a laudatory monograph on Thackeray.

The heart of the contribution which Trollope makes to English periodical literature is captured in several famous phrases of which he is more victim than subject. Henry James may be more elegant than George Moore in his appraisal, but he is hardly more pointed. James writes of Trollope that "his great, his inestimable merit, was a complete appreciation of the usual," while Moore praises him as the man who "carried commonplace further than anyone dreamed it could be carried." It is to Moore, also, that we owe "Trollopy" as the description of Trollope's ponderous, unhurried style.

Dickens makes the remarkable seem commonplace; Trollope makes the commonplace seem worth remarking. As contributor to *Blackwood's* and *Cornhill,* as one of the founders of *Fortnightly Review* (1865), and as first editor of *St. Paul's Magazine* which he joins after retiring from civil service in 1867, Trollope provides a calming antidote to the heightened style of Dickens, his associates, and his imitators.

Passages removed from a novel's context can be used to prove almost anything; certainly it would not be difficult to demonstrate that Dickens was dull by removing a brief section from any one of his novels. Nevertheless, the following selection from *Framley Parsonage* seems to me fairly to epitomize both the Trollope disparaged by James and Moore and the pamphlet-and-magazine novelist who deeply pleased his Victorian audience:

Lady Lufton had but two children. The eldest, a

53

daughter, had been married some four or five years to Sir George Meredith, and this Miss Monsell was a dear friend of hers. And now looms before me the novelist's great difficulty. Miss Monsell—or, rather, Mrs. Mark Robarts—must be described. As Miss Monsell, our tale will have to take no prolonged note of her. And yet we will call her Fanny Monsell, when we declare that she was one of the pleasantest companions that could be brought near to a man, as the future partner of his home, and owner of his heart. And if high principles without asperity, female gentleness without weakness, a love of laughter without malice, and a true loving heart, can qualify a woman to be a parson's wife, then was Fanny Monsell qualified to fill that station. In person she was somewhat larger than common. Her face would have been beautiful but that her mouth was large. Her hair, which was copious, was of a bright brown; her eyes also were brown, and, being so, were the distinctive feature of her face, for brown eyes are not common. They were liquid, large, and full either of tenderness or of mirth. Mark Robarts still had his accustomed luck, when such a girl as this was brought to Framley for his wooing. And he did woo her—and won her. For Mark himself was a handsome fellow. At this time the vicar was about twenty-five years of age, and the future Mrs. Robarts was two or three years younger. Nor did she come quite empty-handed to the vicarage. It cannot be said that Fanny Monsell was an heiress, but she had been left with a provision of some few thousand pounds. This was so settled, that the interest of his wife's money paid the heavy insurance on his life which young Robarts effected, and there was left to him, over and above, sufficient to furnish his parsonage in the very best style of clerical comfort, and to start him on the road of life rejoicing.

From the novelist's intimate intervention in the story

No. 1.   *(Price One Shilling.)*   JANUARY, 1850.

With an Etching by W. HOLMAN HUNT.

The Germ:

Thoughts towards Nature

In Poetry, Literature, and Art.

When whoso merely hath a little thought
    Will plainly think the thought which is in him,—
    Not imaging another's bright or dim,
Not mangling with new words what others taught;
When whoso speaks, from having either sought
    Or only found,—will speak, not just to skim
    A shallow surface with words made and trim,
But in that very speech the matter brought:
Be not too keen to cry—"So this is all!—
    A thing I might myself have thought as well,
    But would not say it, for it was not worth!"
    Ask: "Is this truth?"   For is it still to tell
That, be the theme a point or the whole earth,
Truth is a circle, perfect, great or small?

London:

AYLOTT & JONES, 8, PATERNOSTER ROW.

G. F. TUPPER, Printer, Clement's Lane, Lombard Street.

("And now looms before me the novelist's great difficulty"), to Fanny Monsell's large and liquid brown eyes ("for brown eyes are not common"), to the lucky Mark Robarts ("a handsome fellow") whose new wife's money is sufficient "to start him on the road of life rejoicing," the passage is a Victorian English dream designed to sell magazines (*Cornhill*) at an astonishing rate. Trollope's complete appreciation of the usual, combined with an audience trained to venerate the commonplace, places him second only to Dickens as journalist and novelist in the judgment of his readers.

The work of Thackeray and Trollope concludes this brief examination of some significant English periodicals, their writers, and their editors in the eighteenth and nineteenth centuries. The accompanying list of thirty-nine serial publications contains, however, three very small magazines which are insignificant in the development of the genre but have special importance for the contemporary reader. Earliest of these is *The Germ,* a monthly magazine first appearing on 1 January 1850, whose life is limited to four numbers and two hundred pages. Though it is produced in the same year as *Household Words* and, like Dickens' magazine, published in London and written in English, it has almost no other apparent relationship to the mid-century world of English periodical literature.

The Germ is begun by seven very young men as the voice of their society, the Pre-Raphaelite Brotherhood, itself founded in 1848. Its editor is W. M. Rossetti, younger by a year than his more famous brother, Dante Gabriel, who is also one of the seven. Though Dante dominates *The Germ* and comes to be regarded as spokesman for the Brotherhood, the real founding spirits of both are the painters John Everett Millais and William Holman Hunt. Their original intent is nicely summarized by Mary Bennett in the two opening paragraphs of her "Introduction" to the catalogue of Hunt's paintings for the 1969 exhibition at the Victoria and Albert Museum in London:

> William Holman Hunt's purpose was to use realism and original imagery to express significant moral ideas. To do this he discarded conventional

55

composition and subject matter, and developed a detailed realistic technique. In the process he discovered the importance of the effect of light on color.

The formation of the Pre-Raphaelite Brotherhood in 1848 was largely due to his questioning and rejection of contemporary artistic principles. It aspired to return to nature for a renewal of vitality in painting and to early Italian masters for inspiration. He remained the only member of the Brotherhood to adhere to their principles of detailed realism throughout life, and this placed him in later life in an isolated position in the midst of contemporary art movements and contemporary thought. But while in his youth a rebel with his fellow Pre-Raphaelites, in maturity his paintings came to epitomize for the Victorian the Christian ideal in understandable terms.

Hunt is to Victorian morality in art what Trollope is in literature. But moral explicators who are (even slightly) ahead of their time can suffer indignities at the hands of those they seek to inform and improve. Such especially is the case with Hunt, Millais, and the Rossetti brothers. In 1849 Hunt and Millais are invited to exhibit at the Royal Academy show; they accept, and each sends a picture inscribed with his signature followed by the initials PRB. Each is praised in both *Athenaeum* and *Art Journal,* two of the era's most important critical organs, and little interest is evinced in the signatory initials.

By contrast, the 1850 exhibition at the Royal Academy is held in a radically altered climate of opinion. In the intervening year *The Germ* has happened; part of its purpose is fully to explain the PRB initials by publishing a manifesto for the Brotherhood. Simply speaking, the young artists assert that received opinion of the gods (Rembrandt and Reynolds) is inapplicable to artistic practice in the middle of the nineteenth century; furthermore, those who follow the old gods (all English painters other than members of the

56

THE SAVOY

AN ILLUSTRATED QUARTERLY

No. 2

April 1896

Price **2/6** net

EDITED
BY

ARTHUR
SYMONS

THE SAVOY

AN ILLUSTRATED MONTHLY

No. 3   July 1896   Price **2/-**

EDITED BY ARTHUR SYMONS

AUBREY BEARDSLEY, ETC.

PRB) are dolts. Only the Brothers are surprised when the dolts strike back.

The *Athenaeums* critic writes that "Abruptness, singularity, uncouthness, are the counters with which they play for fame." Not to be outdone, the man from *Art Journal* sneers that "the drawing and manner of the figures show all the objectionable peculiarities of the infancy of Art." Ruskin champions them publicly in the *Times* but the damage is done: Not only will no self-respecting reader of periodical criticism buy their paintings, but *The Germ* itself is discontinued for want of subscribers.

During its brief life, *The Germ* has literary merits of its own to recommend it. William Rossetti is a good editor, an excellent art critic, and a competent poet whose sonnet is published on the cover of the PRB's magazine. After *The Germ* ceases publication, Rossetti goes on to write art criticism for magazines like *The Spectator* and *The Critic*, and art history for the *Encylopedia Brittannica*. While editing *The Germ* he has the good sense to capitalize on his family connections to obtain "The Blessed Damozel" from his brother Dante Gabriel, and "The Dream" from his sister Christina. Together they are the literary highlight of the periodical's brief existence. Later readers have generally regretted its quick demise, for it promised to be one of the most provocative of all English magazines.

Half a century after *The Germ* explicates the doctrine and publishes the poetry and opinions of the Brotherhood, two other small magazines briefly build a by-way in English periodical history. *The Yellow Book* and *Savoy* are *fin de siecle* phenomena chiefly distinguished in the mauve decade by their association with the "Rhymer's Club." Like the Brotherhood, whose most conspicuous member—D. G. Rossetti—is a literary figure and not its real leader, the Club's most notorious member—Oscar Wilde—is a literary man not looked to by the other Rhymers for leadership. Their acknowledged chief is the brilliant, eratic consumptive, Aubrey Beardsley, whose pen is as gifted in line as Wilde's is in language.

In 1894, when Beardsley is not yet twenty-two, he is

invited by publisher John Lane to be art editor of a new illustrated magazine to be called *The Yellow Book*. Brian Reade, in his catalogue notes for the Aubrey Beardsley Exhibition held in 1966 at the Victoria and Albert, describes Beardsley's association with Lane's magazine:

> The appearance of the first number of *The Yellow Book* in April, 1894, brought [Beardsley's] name before the general reading public; but the unprecedented style of the drawings by him reproduced in it, the grotesque portrait of Mrs. Patrick Campbell the actress, his treatment of the theme of Flaubert's novel *L'Education Senti-mentale,* a macabre book-plate design and the *demi-mondaine* Night Piece and cover, all bewildered or disgusted the critics and appealed only to the enlightened among observers. Similar reactions were displayed each time one of the succeeding three numbers of *The Yellow Book* was published. Beardsley had become notorious.

One year and four numbers after Lane engages Beardsley, he is forced by private action and public reaction to sack him. Private action is led by a group of regular contributors to the magazine who refuse to have their writings published in conjunction with Beardsley's drawings. Public reaction occurs in April 1895 when Wilde is arrested after denial of his libel action against the Marquis of Queensberry. Enormous press coverage arouses so much popular feeling against him and his associates that a mob smashes windows in the office of *The Yellow Book* even though Wilde never contributed to it and is piqued at never having been asked.

Beardsley is only briefly unemployed. Arthur Symons, in his book *Aubrey Beardsley,* recalls their first meeting which takes place only a few months after the artist is forced to leave Lane's magazine:

> It was in the summer of 1895 that I first met Aubrey Beardsley. A publisher had asked me to form and edit a new kind of magazine, which was to appeal to the public equally in its letterpress and

its illustrations: need I say that I am defining The Savoy? It was, I admit, to have been something of a rival to The Yellow Book, which by that time had ceased to mark a movement and had come to be little more than a publisher's magazine. I forget exactly when the expulsion of Beardsley from The Yellow Book had occurred; it had been sufficiently recent, at all events, to make Beardsley singularly ready to fall in with my project when I went to him and asked him to devote himself to illustrating my quarterly. He was supposed, just then, to be dying; and as I entered the room, and saw him lying out on a couch, horribly white, I wondered if I had come too late. He was full of ideas, full of enthusiasm, and I think it was then that he suggested the name *Savoy*.

The Savoy runs for a year. Symons and Beardsley attract such authors as Shaw, Beerbohm, Yeats, and Ernest Dowson, and artists like Charles Conder and William Rothenstein. But Wilde's debacle ruins the public's taste for aestheticism while Symons and Beardsley can wear only the color of mauve. One year and a thousand pages after its birth, *The Savoy* expires for want of readers to purchase it.

"If I am not grotesque, I am nothing," says Beardsley of himself. Roger Fry calls him "The Fra Angelico of Satanism." Both views are expanded by Symons in his definition of *fin de siecle* art, a definition which serves as an apt epitaph for *The Yellow Book* and *The Savoy*:

> [It] seeks for sharp, sudden, arresting means of expression....it takes....wilfully and for effect, that beauty which is least evident, indeed least genuine; nearest to ugliness in the grotesque, nearest to triviality in a certain elegant dantiness, nearest also to brutality and the spectacular vices. Art is not sought for its own sake, but the [artist] perfects himself to express a fanciful, ingenious, elaborate, somewhat tricky way of seeing things, which he has deliberately adopted.

Symons' words are an epitaph for all that is grotesque,

dainty, and tricky in English periodical literature through the end of the nineteenth century. A review of any representative portion of these three hundred and fifty thousand selected pages must lead the reader toward the conclusion that normalcy is all. Genuine idiosyncracy in the history of English periodicals is remarkably rare; where it occurs, it is most likely to make a name and mar a fortune.

When Charles Dickens chooses masthead mottoes for his magazines, he twice goes to Shakespeare for the homeliest of phrases: The first time he turns to *Henry V* where he finds the motto that will make the name of his publication "Familiar in [their] mouth[s] as Household Words." The second time he goes to *Othello* and finds "The story of our lives from [year to year]." Both are paraphrases, the changes from "his mouth" to "their mouths" and from "day to day" to "year to year" expressing Dickens' desire for the broad coverage and comprehensive view which are the invariable keynote of sustained success in English periodical publication.

THE SAVOY

No. 1

January

1896

LEONARD SMITHERS

EFFINGHAM HOUSE

ARUNDEL STREET, STRAND

LONDON W.C.

AUBREY
BEARDSLEY.
1896.

Bibliography

All the year round; a weekly journal, conducted by Charles Dickens
   Volumes 1-76 (April 30, 1859-March 1895)

Bee (Oliver Goldsmith)
   Numbers 1-8 (October 6-November 24, 1759)

Bentley's miscellany (Dickens, and others)
   Volumes 1-64 (1837-1868)

British Apollo, or Curious amusements for the ingenious
   Volumes 1-4, number 20 (February 13, 1708-May 11, 1711)

Briton (Smollett)
   Numbers 1-38 (May 29, 1762-February 12, 1763)

Butterfly
   Volumes 1-ns2 (May 1893-February 1894, March 1899-February 1900)

Champion, containing a series of papers, humorous, moral, political, and critical (Fielding)
   Numbers 1-94 (November 15, 1739-June 19, 1740)

Critical review; or, Annals of literature (Smollett)
   Volumes 1-5s5 (January 1756-June 1817)

Director; a weekly literary journal
   Volumes 1-2 (January 24-July 4, 1807)

Dramatic censor, or, Weekly theatrical report
   Volumes 1-4 (January 1800-December 1801)

Edinburgh literary journal; or Weekly register of criticism and belles lettres
   Volumes 1-6 (November 15, 1828-January 14, 1832)

Englishman: being the sequel of the Guardian (Steele)
   Numbers 1-ns38 (October 6, 1713-November 21, 1715)

Examiner (Swift)
   Volumes 1-6 (August 3, 1710-July 26, 1714)

Female spectator
   Volumes 1-4 (April 1744-March 1746)

Germ. Art and poetry. Being thoughts towards nature (W. M. Rossetti)
   Numbers 1-4 (January-May 1850)

Grub-Street journal
   Numbers 1-418 (January 8, 1730-December 29, 1737)

Guardian (Addison and Steele)
   Volumes 1-2 (March 12-October 1, 1713)

Household words. A weekly journal. Conducted by Charles Dickens
   Volumes 1-19 (March 30, 1850-May 28, 1859)

Leigh Hunt's journal; a miscellany for the cultivation of the memorable, the progressive, and the beautiful
   Numbers 1-17 (December 7, 1850-March 29, 1851)

Leigh Hunt's London journal and the printing machine
   Volumes 1-2 (April 2, 1834-December 31, 1835)

Liberal. Verse and prose from the South
   Volumes 1-2 (1822-1823)

Literary gazette. A weekly journal of literature, science and the fine arts
   Volumes 1-ns8 (January 25, 1817-April 26, 1862)

London magazine; or Gentleman's monthly intelligencer
   Volumes 1-ns4 (April 1732-June 1785)

Lover. Written in imitation of the Tatler by Marmaduke Myrtle Gent (Steele)
  Numbers 1-40 (February 25-May 27, 1714)

Macmillan's magazine
  Volumes 1-ns2 (November 1859-October 1907)

Mercator; or, Commerce retrieved (Defoe and others)
  Numbers 1-181 (May 26, 1713-July 20, 1714)

Mirror of the stage; or, New dramatic censor
  Volumes 1-5, number 2 (August 12, 1822-1824)

New London magazine; being an universal and complete monthly repository of knowledge, instruction, and entertainment
  Volumes 1-9, number 6 (July 1785-June 1793)

Present state of the republick of letters
  Volumes 1-18 (January 1728-December 1736)

Rambler (Johnson)
  Numbers 1-208 (March 20, 1750-March 17, 1752)

Saint Paul's magazine (Trollope)
  Volumes 1-14, number 3 (October 1867-March 1874)

Savoy (Symons)
  Numbers 1-8 (January-December 1896)

Spectator (Addison and Steele)
  Volumes 1-8 (March 1, 1711-December 6, 1712, June 18-September 29, 1714)

Tatler (Steele and Addison)
  Numbers 1-271 (April 12, 1709-January 2, 1710 [i.e. 1711])

Theatre; a monthly review and magazine
  Volumes 1-ns39 (1877-1897)

Theatrical inquisitor
  Volumes 1-ns1 (September 1812-November 1820)

Theatrical journal
  Volumes 1-34 (1839-June 4, 1873)

Universal chronicle and weekly gazette (Johnson)
  Numbers 1-105 (April 8, 1758-April 5, 1760)

World
  Volumes 1-4 (January 4, 1753-December 30, 1756)

Yellow book; an illustrated quarterly (Beardsley)
  Volumes 1-13 (April 1894-April 1897)

Index

Chew, Samuel (1888-1960)

Chinese Letters
SEE *Citizen of the World*

Christian Hero (1701)

Fielding, Henry (1707-54)
20, compared to Smollett; Licensing Act of 1737; *Pasquin;*
The Historical Register for 1736; one of the most
The Historical Register for 1736; one of the most
admirable men of his day; epitaph excerpt
21, was a practicing Barrister; *The Champion; The Covent*
Garden Journal; Joseph Andrews; Amelia; History of
Tom Jones; compared to Goldsmith

Forster, John (1812-76)
34, friend to Dickens
36, Dickens writes about new magazine

Fox, Charles James (1749-1806)
13, "The Club"

Fra Angelico of Satinism
SEE Beardsley, Aubrey (p. 59)

Framley Parsonage (1861)
52, appears in *Cornhill Magazine*
53, responsible for *Cornhill's* success; excerpt from

Fraser's Magazine
51, Thackeray

Fry, Roger (1866-1934)
59, on Beardsley

Funeral, The (1701)
1, Steele
2, morality

Garrick, David (1717-79)
13, "The Club"

Gaskell, Elizabeth Cleghorn (1810-65)
37

Lane, John (1854-1925)
  58,   publisher of *The Yellow Book*

Leigh Hunt's Journal (1850-51)
  30

Leigh Hunt's London Journal (1834-35)
  30

Lewis, Clive Staples (1898-1963)
  6,   characterization of Addison

Liberal, The
  27,   beginning of
  30,   end of

Licensing Act of 1737
  20,   Fielding

Life of Samuel Johnson (1791)
  13

Literary club
  13,   Johnson

lite

literary criticism
  6,   Addison as contributor to theory of; numbers 411-421
        of *The Spectator* — brilliant essays on subject of
  16,   excerpt from Johnson's biography of Minim

Literary History of England, A
  47,   excerpt on Dickens

Little Dorrit (1857-58)
  39

London Gazette, The
  7,   includes advertisement for Defoe's arrest